Selling Income Property Successfully

Selling

INCOME PROPERTY

Successfully

JOHN B. ALLEN

Prentice-Hall, Inc.   Englewood Cliffs, N. J.

PRENTICE-HALL INTERNATIONAL, INC., London
PRENTICE-HALL OF AUSTRALIA, PTY. LTD., Sydney
PRENTICE-HALL OF CANADA, LTD., Toronto
PRENTICE-HALL OF INDIA PRIVATE LTD., New Delhi
PRENTICE-HALL OF JAPAN, INC., Tokyo

LIBRARY OF CONGRESS
CATALOG CARD NUMBER: 75–123090

PRINTED IN THE UNITED STATES OF AMERICA
ISBN—0-13-805333-2
B&P

A Word from the Author

This book will enable anyone in the real estate business to succeed in the burgeoning field of income property sales. In that respect it is unique. There is nothing in it about how to list and sell homes. While reading it, you won't have to waste your time trying to convert lessons someone learned in residential sales to the income property sales field.

It is filled with techniques that will make more money for you. These techniques have been learned and proven on the firing line by thousands of successful men in income property sales—techniques that would take you two or three lifetimes to learn by day-to-day experience.

It is a down-to-earth book. The situations are real. The lessons have been extracted from thousands of closed transactions. By learning them you will gain greater confidence; you will become more effective. You will cash more commission checks.

As you read it you will recognize many of the listing and sales situations. They will confirm some of your experience. The complete explanation of the background of these familiar situations will make you stronger. You will be able to use techniques you already know more effectively.

All successful listings and sales are firmly grounded in the fundamental principles of income property sales. One of the sincerest compliments one expert can pay to another is: "He's a good mechanic." That is to say, he understands the fundamentals and applies them as an expert. After reading this book you will be a good mechanic.

It has been said that excellence is the mastery of fundamentals. But fundamentals mastered and not applied are useless. This book shows you how to apply the fundamentals like a master. You will know exactly what to do even in sales situations which seem new to you. You'll handle everything with ease because your knowledge will be built on a firm foundation. It will be a profitable experience for you.

JOHN B. ALLEN

Table of Contents

4 The Listing Process—Your Gold Mine *49*

*The Selling Salesman—49 • Listers Are the Real Sales-
men • The Listing Process—50 • Your Address List •
Assessor's Records Easy to Use • A Treasure House of
Information • How to Contact Sellers • Ten Ways to
Meet the Owner • The Listing Call—54 • One or Two
Calls? • The Two-Call Method • Typical First Call
Problems • Facts Measure Motivation • How to Gather
the Facts • The Second Call—58 • Go See It • Evaluate
the Property • Some Tips on Using Your Evaluation •
Three-Column Analysis • Purpose of Second Call •
Controlling Fear—60 • Believe In Yourself • Don't
Argue • Getting the Signature • Conditioning the
Seller—62 • Offer Problems • Advertising—63 • Points
to Remember—63*

5 How to List Property at the Right Price *65*

*Your Attitude—65 • Work with the Odds • Make a
Trade • You Never Lose • Your Knowledge—67 •
Using Comparable Sales • Using the Income Ap-
proach—69 • Derived Data • The Gross Multiplier •
Percentages • Be Accurate • Talking Price to Your
Seller—70 • The Second Mortgage • The "You Get"
Approach • I Paid More Than That for It! • Points
to Remember—73*

6 Profit-Making Letters *75*

*The Role of Letters—75 • Letters Get It Started •
The Job of a Letter • Three Letters—76 • Recently
Listed Letter • Recently Sold Letters • General Listing
Letter • Success Techniques—80 • Custom Look •
Letter Style • Timing • Follow-up • Copy Comments •
News About Your Neighborhood—82 • Use of Ad-
dresses • Points to Remember—83*

**7 How to Reap the Greatest Benefit
from Your Advertising** *85*

*The Classified Ad—85 • Getting Listings • The Ordi-
nary Ad • Institutionalize Your Ads • A Profit-Making
Edge • Display Ads • Domination • How to Write an*

7 How to Reap the Greatest Benefit from Your Advertising—Continued

8 Profitable Sales Aids and How to Use Them 99

9 Qualifying for Dollars 109

10 Showing Property Successfully 123

Selling Income Property Successfully

1

Your Ninety-Day Success Program— The Key to Income Property Sales

You are an income property salesman. You're not an ordinary salesman. The ordinary ones don't read books like this. You are ready for greater success and you'll have it because you're able to take the success programs and techniques used by other successful real estate men and make them your own. This is your book. The ideas you discover here, combined with the experience you already have, will put thousands of extra dollars in your pocket this year.

There are no magic formulas for instant success in income property sales. Success comes by working smart and by working hard. The top men plan well, prepare thoroughly, discuss completely, execute well, and review everything after they've done it. If there is any formula for success in income property sales, it may be found in these five words: *plan, prepare, discuss, execute* and *review.*

The ninety-day success program that is laid out at the end of this chapter is built around those five key words. It shows you, step-by-step, exactly what you must do to improve your present level of performance. It is a pattern of action, a program that insures continued and increasing success. It is the "what to do." The balance of the book shows you "how to do it."

Planning

Don't be misled by the references to careful planning and meticulous attention to detail stressed throughout this book. Income property selling is an *action* business—action preceded by the bare minimum of detailed planning.

Your job is not to plan—your job is to list and sell. Planning is not an end; it is your means to an end. Too many promising careers have been smashed on the rocks of great plans. Don't make yours the next one.

Keep planning in its place. Do it when required. Make your planning efficient. Force it into a strict time allotment. If you're not jealous of the time given to planning, you can become a slave to it; you can become a planner, not a doer.

With practice, all essential planning can be done with efficiency and dispatch. Many plans are self perpetuating (your listing plan, for example) and, once conceived, can serve you well for many months or years. Success-program salesmen know this truth. Their plans almost always have more than one use. By getting multiple use out of most things they do, success-program brokers lower their cost, in time, and increase their earnings.

Failure Signals

Many men work hard, yet they fail. It is one of life's realities that hard work does not always guarantee success. It is a tragedy of real estate sales management that so many willing workers are allowed to work so hard doing the wrong things.

You will find references to failure signals as you study each chapter. Think of them as red lights. Every time you come to one, stop and think. Knowing the failure signals can make you as much money as knowing the success program.

It is a failure signal, for example, to carry out a listing call when you're not talking to all of the owners at once. Similarly, you are facing a failure signal when you try to present an offer to only one owner if there are two owners of the property. Watch for the failure signals. Stop at each one and think.

The Examples

There are many examples in the book. All of them are true. They are used to illustrate how the success-program broker handles the particular situation being discussed. Many of them are actual sales talks. Don't try to memorize these presentations. Study them and get the concept. Once you have the idea put the sales talk in your own words. When it's you, it will work. If you're merely an actor delivering lines you might entertain, but you'll seldom sell.

ORGANIZATION OF THE BOOK

This book is organized along the lines of your success program. Chapter 2 deals with your personal success package. Chapters 3 through 6 are devoted to the listing process. Chapters 7 through 15 are about sales. There is one valuable chapter on exchanging, which will do much to influence your thinking on this area of your business. The last chapter has tips on how to work with attorneys, accountants, lenders and other brokers; this skill is valuable in both listing and selling.

Your Personal Success Package

The single most important aspect of your success is you. In Chapter 2 you'll find valuable ideas on how to develop a successful personal package. This chapter is the foundation upon which you can continue to build a successful income property career.

Your attitude, how you think about yourself and your work, is of critical importance. No one can hand you a set of success attitudes. This book tells you the kind of viewpoints successful men have. It's up to you to take these attitude ideas and make them work for you. Think of them as the seeds of a successful career. Make your mind the fertile ground in which they can grow.

The Listing Process

Listings are like air. Without them you die. There are four chapters devoted to this vital subject. Read and re-read these chapters until the concepts presented are so deeply ingrained that they become reflex actions.

Here are some examples of the concepts to be found in the listing chapters:

    —This is a listing business.
    —The object of taking a listing is to get a sale; it is not to get an offer.
    —The purpose of all advertising is to get listings.

As you study this section, make a list of the fundamental concepts of real estate that you find. Then, live by these fundamentals.

The Selling Process

The selling process appears last, because sales are the natural, predictable result of taking good listings. When you've got good property for sale, buyers will find you. This is true in good times or bad.

Success-program salesmen like to meet and deal with buyers. But buyers are seen in their proper place. That place is at the end of a very long line. It's surprising how often a friend, knowing you're in the income property business, will come up to you and, in an excited voice, say: "I've got a customer for you. He's got $50,000 and he wants to buy some income property!"

Great news. It's like the friend of a banker saying, "I've got a customer for you. He wants to borrow $50,000!" The banker seldom needs borrowers; he needs depositors. The income property salesman seldom needs buyers; he always needs sellers.

YOUR NINETY-DAY SUCCESS PROGRAM

There are many roads to success. Here are six of them, three routes to follow for listings, three for sales. They are the most effective paths to consistent, high earnings.

How to Use Them

Each success-program is set up to be worked separately in 90-day time segments. One of the underlying ideas is to help you build a longer range view of your activity than that usually held by the salesman on a failure course. The man who fails lives from day to day. He seldom looks even one month ahead. I've never known a failure who could see 90 days ahead.

Each program is meant to be used over and over. All of them require 90 days of all-out, intensive effort. When you complete one 90-day program, start another one. Each 90-day period builds for the future. In the listing program (method one), for example, the 150 to 200 properties you develop in your first quarter will be added to the 150 to 200 properties you gather in the second quarter. After four 90-day periods, you will have a file of 600 to 800 potential listings, or four times the chance to succeed, than you had in the first quarter.

You might work more than one method at a time. Some success-program salesmen do. It takes a high degree of experience and dedication to work several listing and selling programs at once. If you try it, ask yourself, "Am I doing many things poorly rather than one thing well?"

90-DAY PROGRAM

A. Listing

1. Method Number One—Mail

STEP ONE— *Set up listing areas.*
Goal: Fifteen areas containing not less than 15 properties each. Record property addresses and ownership data on PERMANENT record cards.

STEP TWO— *Listing letters.*
Mail listing solicitation letter (general letter, recently listed or recently sold) to each owner in your listing area. Send out in groups of 20–25 letters.

STEP THREE—*Replies*
Wait for response to listing letters.
a) When you get a reply make an appointment to list.
b) If no reply contact owners by telephone and, where practical, in person.
Discuss merits of letter follow-up with your manager; pay special attention to: time requirement, distance involved, entries on permanent record card.

STEP FOUR— *The listing call.*
Make at least two listing calls with your manager or broker.
First call—manager handles the call, you observe.
Second call—you handle the call, manager observes.
Discuss two-call method with manager.
Give special attention to PREPARATION for a listing call.

STEP FIVE— *Review.*
Discuss each listing call with your manager. Direct your attention to both the strengths and weaknesses of your calls.

STEP SIX— *Independent work.*
Make at least 15 listing appointments. Go on them by yourself. Pay special attention to your preparation for each call—do you know what you're talking about? Discuss each listing call with your manager both before and after the call. This

is often missed by experienced men. If you ever
hit a slump, review this step.

STEP SEVEN— *Servicing.*

    a) Set up your listing file.

    b) Follow a step-by-step listing service procedure.
Note how many pieces of information on the
property you are missing. This step is an important checkpoint; it should indicate how
carefully you took the listing.

STEP EIGHT— *Sales meeting pitch.*

Present not less than five of your properties to
your fellow salesmen in your sales meeting (one
listing pitch per meeting).

Note: This step should be taken:

a) when listed, and

b) when extended, reduced or changed in any
substantial way.

STEP NINE— *Price reduction.*

Set up a price reduction call on one of your listings. Thoroughly prepare your case. Take your
manager on at least one price reduction call.

STEP TEN— *Extension.*

This is not ordinarily an activity required within
90 days—most listings are 180 days. You should,
when appropriate, ORGANIZE YOUR LISTING
FILE and prepare a campaign to get an extension.
Work closely with your manager in the planning
stage and take him with you on at least one extension call.

2. Method Two—By Owner

STEP ONE— *Your list.*

Step up a list of not less than 25 for sale by owner
properties. Gather your data from:

a) signs on property.

b) classified ads (use ads one month old).

STEP TWO— *Contact.*

Organize a personal telethon. Call each of your
for sale by owners. Try doing this in the evening.
Get at least two listing appointments.

STEP THREE—*The listing call.*

Go on two calls with your manager. Follow procedure outlined under Listing Method One from
Step Four through Step Ten.

3. Method Three—Expired Listings
   STEP ONE—   *Your list.*
                Set up a list of not less than 50 expired listings.
   STEP TWO—   *Contact.*
                Contact each owner on your list by
                a) mail
                b) telephone
                c) in person.
                Discuss merits of each contact method with your
                manager. Make at least five appointments to list.
   STEP THREE—*The listing call.*
                Follow procedure shown under Listing, Method
                Number One—Mail, from Step Four through
                Step Ten.

B. *Selling*

1. Method Number One—Floor Time
   STEP ONE—   *Your preparation.*
                a) Review proper preparation for floor time with
                   manager. Give special attention to:
                   1. seeing property advertised.
                   2. knowing the ads—read them, BEFORE you
                      get a call.
                   3. showing problems.
                   4. possible switches.
                   5. Review telephone technique.
                      Discuss handling calls with your manager.
                      Give special attention to:
                      a. initial greetings
                      b. complimenting buyer for calling
                      c. a sense of excitement and immediacy
                      d. the policy on giving out addresses
                      e. the policy on mailing out set-up sheets
                      f. handling broker calls
                      g. taking messages
                      h. the purpose of an ad call
                Organize some other work to do between ad calls.
   STEP TWO—   *Handling ad calls.*
                Work with the manager at your desk on at least
                   two occasions each quarter.
                a) Listen while manager handles several ad calls.
                b) Let manager listen while you handle several
                   ad calls.

STEP THREE—*Discussion.*

Review your add calls with your manager. Discuss both strengths and weaknesses of each call. Pay special attention to:

a) your attitude

b) how closely you follow ad call procedures.

STEP FOUR— *Talk-ins.*

Set a goal for each floor day to make at least one appointment to show property. A good standard is to make an appointment on at least 50% of your ad calls. (Your goal is 100%.) If your appointment percentage falls below 50% review with your manager.

STEP FIVE— *Showing.*

Show 15 to 20 clients 45–60 properties in this 90 days.

a) Have your manager go with you on a showing.

b) Discuss results. Pay special attention to:

1. qualifying

2. preparation to show

3. successful showing techniques

4. closing methods

STEP SIX— *Offers.*

Write at least six offers. Ask for manager assistance on one or two of these. Review:

1. the order blank close

2. deposit receipt phraseology

STEP SEVEN— *Presentation.*

Take manager with you on one offer presentation. Review:

1. preparation

2. role of listing salesman

3. methods of presenting offer

4. making appointment

STEP EIGHT—*Inspection.*

Prepare carefully. Discuss inspection procedure with manager. If convenient, have manager go with you on at least one property inspection. Review:

1) setting up inspection with owner

2) rental statement

3) personal property inventory

4) getting approval of property

STEP NINE—   *Closing details.*
Review your sales follow-up check list procedure with manager. Get manager to help open at least one closing procedure. In your discussion with manager pay special attention to:
1) financing—application, beneficiary statements, costs
2) rental statement
3) bill of sale—inventory procedure
4) relations with person handling mechanics of title transfer
5) how to follow-up and service
6) getting funds in to close.

STEP TEN—   *Follow-up.*
Review after-sale service with manager. Pay special attention to:
1) getting closing statement out promptly
2) getting checks out promptly
3) visit to property with new owner if appropriate
4) call on seller (if your listing) to get LISTING prospects
5) recently sold letters.

2. Method Number Two—Former clients.

STEP ONE—   *Your list.*
Set-up a list of former buyers or prospects. This list should contain at least 50 names. Use:
a) closed sales files
b) old prospect cards

STEP TWO—   *Contact.*
Call each of these prospects. Discuss method to be used in your calls with your manager. Make appointment to show property. Set aside Thursday, or Friday night for a personal buyer telethon. Objective: to set-up at least 4 appointments to show property over the weekend.

STEP THREE—*Showing*
Show at least 5 of these 50 former clients' property. Discuss the 3-property showing method with your manager. Use it on all 5 showings. Pay special attention to:
closing techniques.

STEP FOUR—   *Offers.*
Set a goal of two offers. Follow procedure out-

lined in selling Method Number One, Floor Time from Step Six through Step Ten.

3. Method Number Three—Creative.

STEP ONE— *Getting it started.*

a) General

Mention that you are an income property salesman to at least 100 people in 90 days. Give out your card. Ask the three magic questions:
1. do you want to sell?
2. do you want to buy?
3. do you know anyone who wants to buy or sell?

b) Specific.

Make a list of 15 attorneys, 15 doctors, 15 accountants. (Use the yellow pages or professional directories.)

STEP TWO— *Selection.*

Pick out a good property to sell.

STEP THREE—*Contact.*

Discuss contact method with manager then:
1. Call each attorney, doctor and accountant.
2. Tell him about your good buy. If not interested ask him if he wants to sell any property.
4. Make appointment to show the property.

STEP FOUR— *Showing.*

Show at least 5 of these 45 prospects the target property. Discuss with manager:
1. tax benefit analysis
2. five-year ownership projection.

Prepare at least two of these presentations. Use them on your calls. Review:
1. qualifying techniques
2. closing methods.

STEP FIVE— *Offers.*

Set a goal of at least two offers. Follow procedure outlined in selling, Method One—Floor Time, from Step Six through Step Ten.

90-DAY RESULTS	
A. LISTING	**B. SELLING**
1. Number of listing areas _____	1. Client telethons (Thursday & Friday _____
2. Number of properties in listing area _____	2. Property shown _____
3. Number of letters sent _____	3. Offers written _____
4. Number of listing calls _____	4. Sales made _____
5. Number of listings taken _____	
6. Number of reductions _____	
7. Number of extensions _____	
8. Number of listings sold _____	

Easier Said Than Done?

It's easy to outline such programs. Can they be accomplished? Absolutely. But, they are easier said than done.

The balance of this book shows you exactly how to do it. If you adopt these success programs this is the minimum result you may expect in one year.

You will take 36 listings. You will have 25–30 of those listings sell. You will make 12–15 sales on your own.

You will be in the upper 10%, in earnings, in your profession.

2

Developing Your
Personal Success Package

Selling real estate is one thing; selling income property success-fully is another. A successful income property salesman has dis-tinguished himself in an intricate and challenging business. The distinction between him and the ordinary real estate salesman lies, to a great extent, in his close attention to developing and maintaining a personal success package.

CAREER CONSCIOUSNESS

It may seem odd, even out of place, to speak of career consciousness in a book written for experienced income property salesmen. You have made your choice. You're already in the business.

Let me explain myself. I have been managing income property salesmen for almost ten years. In that time I've been associated with many successful men. All those who succeeded were experienced. Many of these successful men later failed. Why? Among those who failed, there was always one missing ingredient: They lacked a sense of career.

Success is not measured by one good year. Most of the men of whom I speak put two, three, even four good years together before disappearing from the scene. They were just passing through; skim-ming the cream, so to speak.

Most of them had a mental ace in the hole. They lacked true dedication or commitment to income property sales as a career. They had an excuse, not a reason for being in this wonderful business. Ever hear this?

"I'm retired, I just do this to keep busy," or "I have other income," or perhaps, "I'm just doing this until I get my broker's license."

Talk to any man who makes such statements while he takes bundles of money out of his activity and he'll swear he's serious about what he is doing. After all, he's experienced, he's doing well, he's succeeding!

But success is an elusive and fleeting thing, doubly so in income property sales. Many grasp it today, hold it for a while, and then quietly slip into the ranks of the ordinary salesman.

Few stay as top producers for the majority of their business life. Those who achieve success, and keep it, are those who have a deep sense of career. They make a commitment and they make it proudly. Their personal success package is complete.

This is the message I want to communicate to you, an experienced man: Be sensitive to the commitment you've made to your career; guard it carefully.

Personal Strength

You must be mentally and physically strong to achieve maximum success. Your clientele is strong. They have risen to the top of the American investment public. They are in the minority, just as you are. They did not reach the position they now enjoy by being weak. They respect personal strength. To deal with them successfully, you must be strong. Strength respects strength—it abhors weakness.

Your clients are men of conviction. To do business with them you must be a man of conviction. You must stand for something. Success-program salesmen think their positions through and stick with the decisions they know are right.

For example, if you decide that $65,000 is a fair price for a piece of property and you recommend that price to your buyer, you ought to stick to your belief in that price. If the buyer wants to offer $62,000, it is your job, based on the strength of your conviction, to convince him to pay $65,000.

An ordinary salesman would write the $62,000 offer just to get the buyer down on paper. Successful men don't do that. It shows weakness. It indicates a lack of belief in your own recommendation, to collapse and give in just because a buyer doesn't immediately agree with you. You must fight for what you know is right. To do otherwise is weak and weakness always loses.

Physical and mental strength go together. A man who is physically drained by inattention to matters of health can't be mentally strong. As Vince Lombardi, the famous football coach, has said: "Fatigue makes cowards of us all."

Continuous Preparation

You were not always the success you are today. As you struggled for a permanent place in income property sales, you spent a lot of time in the classroom and with the books. When it comes to preparation, your personal success package will never be complete. To develop it fully, you must be an information hog.

Knowledge is the fuel of your career. No piece of information, however small, is too slight for your full attention. The big producer pursues every scrap of product and sales knowledge. He runs toward training, not away from it. Don't let your success rob you of the good habits you developed on the way up. Never neglect your professional growth. When you stop learning, you start taking things out of your success package, and you start getting smaller.

Reading

Because of the nature of income property selling, you'll probably seldom handle more than twenty or twenty-five transactions per year. That's four hundred to five hundred in twenty years. With that much transaction experience you can't possibly learn what you must know on the firing line.

You've got to learn from others. Success-program salesmen constantly read books like this one and all the professional literature they can find. Reading adds to your power, it helps keep you mentally alert. It keeps you flexible in your thinking.

Service

When you watch a good income property salesman at work, you can't help but wonder: Is he a salesman or a service man? The really great ones have a highly developed sense of service to their clients. It often appears that they concentrate more on client service than they do on salesmanship. Their transactions seem to be a natural outcome of an avalanche of service.

Complete, accurate, detailed service is a way of life for them. It is the fabric of their careers. They are masterful salesmen, of course, but like all great masters their skills are seldom obvious.

MAINTAIN A GOOD ATTITUDE

Attitude is a matter of constant concern both for the beginner and the old hand. Without a proper attitude you can't succeed or stay successful. When an experienced salesman gets into trouble, when the transactions come hard, it is often because his attitude toward himself or his business has changed.

Those who reach the top and stay there are masters at keeping themselves sold on what they are doing. It's easy to view all sellers as time wasters and all buyers as unrealistic, but it's a personal disaster to let such thinking get a hold on you.

Experienced, successful men often fall into another attitude trap: that of criticizing their company. It's as if they kept all negative thinking dammed up as they got themselves established. Then, having reached a good level of production, the floodgates open; they begin to take advantage of their new stature by brutally pointing out every deficiency they can find in the company's operation. Don't let it happen to you. Remind yourself: There is no perfect job and there is no perfect company. A demanding, criticizing, unreasonable salesman hurts only himself. Make this your rule: Don't criticize unless you have a suggestion to solve the problem.

Reverse Selling

Never lose your sense of adventure. Many good men are lost to income property selling each year because of boredom. Actually, it's not boredom that's responsible for the loss of the high producers; it is *reverse selling*.

When you start earning in the 50% plus tax bracket, you're in dangerous country. Your attitude can cost you your career. Making money seemingly becomes so easy that the challenge, the adventure of it is lost. What happens to you is this: You start talking yourself out of a good thing. Reverse selling sets in. You see deals made routinely and easily. You see personal tax problems. You see huge one-time profits made by principals. And you see yourself as "out of it" as far as the big money is concerned.

All at once you start seeing greener fields. Developing looks like the way to go. The challenge of an untried business becomes irresistible. Your own success seems meager. It's time for a change.

The change you need most is a change in your viewpoint. You've become so good a salesman, you're about to sell yourself right out of business.

YOU ARE A BUSINESSMAN

If there are any differences between ordinary real estate selling and income property selling (and the real differences are few) they may be found in the kind of people you deal with. You have your share of "Momma and Poppa" customers, of course, but the real money is made in dealing with business and professional men. Your typical buyer or seller is a man of considerable experience. He may not always be heavily experienced in real estate (although an ability to deal with the big professional client is becoming more important) but he does have a better than average education and he has the thought patterns and habits of the successful man.

The Businessman

You must be a businessman to deal with him. The businessman is both a visionary and a doer. Because of this seeming conflict (between dreaming and doing) you can approach him with both strong emotional and logical appeals. In general, you must have the skill to show him the big dream first and then back it up with both-feet-on-the-ground logic. One of the biggest differences between the ordinary salesman and the successful salesman is the way the successful one uses the emotions to sell.

Thinking and Acting As a Businessman

The rise to the top in income property sales is a slow one. It generally takes about four years for a well equipped man fresh from college to enter the $30,000 plus earnings bracket. That time can be reduced by 50% or more, for a similarly educated man who has five to ten years of general business experience. The difference lies in the experience background.

You must be able to respond to businessmen; that means thinking and acting like one. It's an essential ingredient of your personal success package. It is difficult to do this without adequate exposure to the world of business.

Flexible Thinking

Successful men have learned how to think. They know that, in any given situation, there are usually several paths to success. They are used to examining the alternatives in an effort to find the route most likely to succeed. They are receptive to changing their approach if the road they are following suddenly becomes blocked. Flexibility is their watchword.

Flexibility is the magic in your personal success package. It is responsible, in large part, for the success you enjoy today. Yet, the older you get, the more experienced and successful you become, the more difficult it is to remain flexible in your thinking.

The real estate business (all of it, not just income property selling) will change more in the next five years than it has in the last fifty. The big lenders aren't big lenders anymore; they're big investors, they're your partners or your competitors.

Big professional buyers are appearing on the scene. Major corporations are going into the ownership and development of real estate. They're after big profits with big money and big plans.

These new forces in the real estate world demand new responses from you. You've got to get bigger, better, more flexible, more professional than ever before if you want to continue to justify your position as the essential ingredient in income property sales. It will take all the flexibility you can muster to devise new approaches to meet these new situations.

Force Activity

To earn a lot of money you must have a lot of activity. It is part of your personal success package to keep many balls in the air at once. All successful income property salesmen do this. One of the best I've ever known said he could easily handle ten major deals simultaneously.

You must force activity. Don't be afraid to have five or six sales in various stages of closing while you work on five or six new ones. The ninety-day success program in Chapter 1 forces lots of activity. If you stake your earning power on one or two bigs deals a year, you'll eventually fail. Just as a good company has many product lines, you must have many deals working.

Pure activity is not enough. You've got to be in on some sizeable transactions. You simply can't make big money without big deals. Many who enjoy moderate success today could be leaders in income property sales if they'd just hook into a few major transactions. It's not hard to do. Just use the little deals to give you walking-around money; work on the big ones to put yourself on the top of the heap.

SUCCESS TECHNIQUES

Those who get the most in material reward and personal satisfaction from income property sales all have one thing in common: They have outstanding success habits. They are able to generate their own activity, they get a lot of practice, they have careful listing policies, they do it the easy way and they avoid gimmicks.

Do It Yourself

It is part of your personal success package to be able to generate your own activity. The man who routinely takes his floor time and depends upon his company to provide him with listing and sales leads, is never the top gun. You can be a very competent man, well able to handle most situations, but if you try to live off your company, you're not going to live very well.

To profit most from your business, you must be a deal maker. You've got to be the one who spots the vacant ground and puts it together with your community's need for a shopping center. And when you do it, stay in the situation from A to Z; get a commission on the sale of the land, the leasing and the final sale of the project to an investor.

A project like that can generate two to three hundred thousand dollars in commissions. Such opportunities are seldom handed to you; they are created by a man who knows how to generate his own activity.

Get Lots of Practice

Your personal success package must include a plan that forces you to get a lot of practice. The men who fail at income property selling are expert at avoiding opportunities to practice their skills. They have no success program. You can't expect to get sharp and stay sharp if you don't practice your techniques. If doctors practiced their operations as seldom as some men practice listing and selling, most of us would be dead.

Welcome the Tough Call

Too many men avoid the "tough call." You know the kind I mean. It's the one where the seller has never given an exclusive listing. Or the one on the guy who won't list for more than thirty days.

It is better to try, and fail on a "tough call" than to succeed on an easy one. Only these difficult situations put your skills to the test. After a few really difficult calls, it's surprising how much easier the normal sales situation becomes. It is also surprising how many times you'll find yourself able to sell the tough customer. Perhaps all he is waiting for is another tough customer to do business with.

One caution: Don't make a career out of one problem. Every sales situation can be solved by someone, but it sometimes proves to be too costly a victory. Your own good judgement will signal when you're in such a situation. When you hear the signal, get out.

Careful Listing Policies

Good salesmen have good listing policies. They have a high regard for the exclusive listing. It is part of their success package to pick and choose among the available listings. It is not unusual for high-earnings men to list only one or two of every ten listings they are offered.

Your attitude toward listing must be correct. You can afford to wait until the time, price or motivation to sell is right. Most of the really good listings are obtained by competent salesmen after some (or many) ordinary salesmen have taken the property on and failed.

Do It the Easy Way

The "loner" seldom makes much money. The man who succeeds in income property sales knows how to work with others. He has lots of partners and lots of deals.

Get involved in transactions with many other salesmen. This is one of the easiest ways of keeping many balls in the air at once. It's a key to the big money. If you play it close to the vest, always depending on your own time and talent, you are severely limiting your earning power.

Look for the easy way. Work with the man who knows about the seller or the buyer. It is wasteful to duplicate work already done by a co-worker or outside broker. Get on the team. Use their skills and information. It's easier to make five deals with others (and get a piece of each one) than to make one deal on your own.

Avoid Gimmicks

The clever devices and techniques that often come to our attention (such as pat closing methods, unusual financing arrangements, cute contact methods) are out of place in your personal success package. They are avoided by the top-earnings men who make income property sales pay off.

The outstanding successes in our field know that there are only two tricks that work: honesty and hard work.

POINTS TO REMEMBER

—Successful income property salesmen succeed on purpose, not by accident.
—You belong to a high-earning minority of real estate salesmen.
—Guard your career commitment carefully.
—You must be mentally and physically strong to stay on top.
—Knowledge is the fuel of your career.
—The big successes are big readers.
—Don't let reverse selling beat you.
—Force lots of activity; keep many balls in the **air.**
—Keep your thinking flexible.
—Get lots of practice.
—Hold on to your careful listing policies.
—Do it the easy way.
—Avoid gimmicks.

3

An Exclusive Listing Policy
for Maximum Success

There is a pattern to our business which you can follow to success. The most essential element of that success pattern is taking listings.

You will never learn a greater truth about income real estate than the one contained in this sign:

> ### THIS IS
> ### A
> ### LISTING BUSINESS

It is not a selling business. If you will take this truth and make it a part of you it will be worth a thousand times the price of this book.

LISTINGS = SALES

The rule that *listings = sales* is well established in every successful home brokerage business. Income property brokers have generally failed to adopt this principle. And what has happened? The home brokerage business has had years of phenomenal growth, while the average income property broker still seeks to grope his way out of the dark ages. He will never see daylight until he decides that, in this respect, there is no difference between home brokerage and income property brokerage. Both are a listing business.

The problem of listing is not that most income salesmen don't believe that *listings = sales*. It is much more subtle. After all, how could anyone in his right mind deny the truth of this general proposition? We all KNOW that *listings = sales*. The problem really is that the majority of us feel ANY listing will equal a sale.

The serious income property salesman must get that false idea out of his mind because it is the greatest failure signal of them all. In the long run, only one class of listing leads to a consistent sales record. That is the exclusive listing.

If you've never heard of open listings, verbal listings, handshake listings or other forms of non-exclusive listings, you are uncommonly lucky and you can skip the balance of this chapter. But if you've heard of, or worked on, any of these non-exclusive arrangements, you're in trouble. You'd better read this chapter twice to guarantee yourself long-term success. You must eradicate from your mind, forever, all thought of working on any property on which you or the cooperating broker does not have a full-term, written, exclusive listing. The company or the man that works on "opens" is on a failure course. It is only a question of time before the door closes forever on his business or career. It's a basic truth of our business.

The Standard Exclusive

Most of us, through our company or our local board, have a standard, printed form for the purpose of taking an exclusive listing —this, basically, is the agreement I am referring to when I say "exclusive." There are, however, a few fine points that merit discussion if you are to profit most from this device.

First, the agreement ought to be not only exclusive but irrevocable. Making the agreement irrevocable automatically makes it more serious. Both the seller and the broker will give more thought to approving an exclusive and irrevocable listing. This extra thought, and the inevitable discussion that stems from it, will contribute to greater confidence between the parties. This is true even in the case where the law provides a seller with the right to revoke an "irrevocable" listing.

Second, your agreement ought to be for at least 180 days. It takes time to sell an income property. Anything less than 180 days diminishes your chance of a sale and your opportunity to earn a commission. And, after all, if two people decide to do business with each other, they ought to think in terms of a long-term relationship. Short,

30- or 60-day listings are really indications of a lack of seller confidence in the broker.

Third, there ought to be a client registration provision. The broker should be protected, as to his registered buyers, for at least 90 days after the expiration date of the exclusive listing. This registration should apply to all persons to whom the property has been *presented* during the term of the listing. Most standard exclusive listings provide for such client registration only to those persons *shown* the property by the broker. The vital difference between *shown* and *presented* is immediately apparent. It is an important and sensible difference to the profit-minded income property salesman. To properly accomplish the client registration, your agreement should provide for this being done, in writing, during the term of the listing or within five days after its expiration. In the absence of local board rules to the contrary, client registration does not bind other brokers who later take an exclusive on the property unless such clients are specifically exempted from their listing.

THE PARTIES TO A TRANSACTION

There are, basically, three parties to every real estate transaction: the buyer, the seller, and the broker. Until all of these parties have their wants and their needs substantially satisfied, no transaction can occur. The interests of all three parties are better served by an exclusive listing than by any other method yet devised.

The Buyer

The buyer expects that the broker will be able to deliver the property to him if he decides to buy it. This is almost always possible when the broker has an exclusive; it is less than a 50–50 possibility if the broker doesn't have an exclusive.

To put it quite simply, most of us invite (through ads) buyers to come in and do business with us. The open listing makes a travesty of this invitation. Millions of buyers have been disappointed by brokers who advertise property they don't control. The offering of open listings is so common, many income property buyers ask "Do you have an exclusive on this property?" You seldom hear a home buyer ask that question.

Buyers are disenchanted with sloppy, open-listing brokers. They are tired of wasting their time trying to buy property that was sold days, or weeks, before their offer was taken. It is interesting to note that buyers have become sick of open, non-exclusive listings before many brokers have. Apparently most buyers place a higher value on their time than do most brokers.

The Seller

Buyers want to do business with a broker who has the confidence of the seller as evidenced by an exclusive listing. Motivated sellers will capitalize on this buyer desire.

Occasionally a buyer will check with the owner after being introduced to the property by a broker. Nothing strengthens your position more than to have the buyer told, "Please check with my broker, he has an exclusive." This statement firmly establishes the essential third-party role of the broker. From the seller's viewpoint, a strong broker is vital. Only in this way, through a strong third party, can the seller get a maximum price for his property.

With an exclusive, the broker can take the time necessary to fashion the best possible offer for his seller. The broker's position is strong. He can speak with authority on behalf of his seller. He can insist on the buyer's best offer the first time. He can fight for this top-dollar offer because he has taken the time to gain the seller's confidence and, in the process, he has learned exactly what his seller wants and needs from the transaction.

With an exclusive, the negotiations are simplified because the broker can take the time to get the buyer's best "shot" the first time. This tends to eliminate the protracted haggling characterized by offer, counter-offer, counter-counter-offer, ad nauseam, which usually leads to "no sale" anyway. A broker with an "open" will write any offer the buyer wants to make. Why not? He's just one runner in a massive foot race.

More sales fail for incomplete or inaccurate information than for any other reason. From the seller's viewpoint, the exclusive is important not for what it is but for what it does. It generally leads to the broker having complete information on the property. No broker who insists on an exclusive is going to leave the seller without complete, accurate data on the property.

The exclusive indicates something else to a thoughtful seller. It shows how serious and professional you really are. Successful, professional brokers won't work without an exclusive. Opportunists will tackle anything. Most sellers expect a careful, conscientious job. They can demand it if they have entered into an exclusive listing with you. Without an exclusive, the seller is lucky if he can get his broker on the telephone.

No property will ever sell until some top-flight broker cares about it. What are the seller and the broker saying to each other when they enter into an open listing agreement? The seller is saying, "I don't care about you, Mr. Broker"; and the broker replies (by taking such a listing), "I don't care about you, either, Mr. Seller." Such a situation is against the best interests of both seller and broker.

In fact, from this "I don't care" attitude stems the confusion in the weak broker's mind as to whom he is really working for. When an exclusive is taken, all confusion melts away. The strong, professional broker works for his seller; that's the party he has a written agreement with. It's no secret. Buyers know it. The only mystery is that so many brokers don't know who they are working for. An exclusive removes all doubt and, in this respect, favors the interest of buyer, seller and broker.

Without an "ex," the broker is tempted to favor the buyer. This weakens the chance for a sale. It robs the buyer of an enthusiastic, intelligent and partisan presentation of the merits of the investment. It sets up a conspiracy between the buyer and the broker against the seller, rather than a cooperative effort to effect a sale.

An exclusive helps the seller think straight. Too many times, where a seller has scattered open listings around, he is faced with an almost impossible decision-making situation. Here it is: The open listing broker stumbles across an offer. He takes it to the seller. Meanwhile the competing seller (real estate salesman par excellent) has been talking with many "interested" buyers. Now you have it. The broker has a written offer. The seller has hopes. Greed rears its ugly head. The seller wants a sale without a commission. Any day now, perhaps today, one of the seller's prospects is going to make an offer. So the seller delays. He doesn't accept the broker's offer. (After all, a day or two won't hurt, will it?) No other offers appear. The broker's buyer disappears. The broker wasn't as much a fool as the seller thought he was; he took his buyer somewhere else. Exit sale and enter an exclusive listing for some other broker. Tell this story to your listing prospects and, more often than not, you'll walk out with your exclusive.

The Broker

Here's another truth to fit into your success-program philosophy: Buyers are sellers. Think, then, in view of this truth, what you are doing to your future when you try to merchandise an open listing. The odds are 99.9 to 1 that the buyer will find out you've only got an "open." Even if you make the sale, what have you done? You've created a monster! You will never get an exclusive from that buyer. Actions speak louder than words and this buyer has already seen you in action. You're an open listing broker.

Non-exclusive listings waste your time and cost you money. The broker who works on "open," verbals and handshakes is a nervous, harried man. He is never quite sure if a property is still available. A telephone call to the seller every five minutes won't even help him be sure he's got anything to sell.

The open-listing artist seldom has an exact idea as to the seller's price or terms. How often have you heard the seller say one or more of these things after getting an offer on an open:

    —I sold it last week.
    —It's interesting that you should bring me an offer today. Why just yesterday (he opens his desk drawer and looks in) I received another offer. In many ways, I like it better. (Pause) What did you say your commission was?
    —Well, that's fine Jack, but this is my net price. I told you you'd have to get your commission on top of that.

Nobody who respects himself or his business is going to be content to live through very many experiences like those. Only the opportunist, the fast-buck guy, will continue to work in such impossible circumstances. The career-conscious man eventually decides to work for only those sellers who want and need his service. The best evidence a seller both wants and needs you is the exclusive listing.

What if it's impossible to get an exclusive? You know some of the typical situations:

    —This man is facing foreclosure. He can't give an exclusive. Fine! Let him sell it himself or go get an ex from the mortgage holder.
    —This man has never given an ex. Small wonder! No one has ever earned one. Give it a try. If you fail, leave it, as an open, to your competition. It'll keep them busy while you sell your other exclusives.
    —This is an estate matter. It's against the law to give an exclusive. Maybe it is. If it is, pass it up. You've got better things to do. But in many states it is not against the probate code to give an exclusive. It is only a violation to give a listing which is not subject to the appropriate court's approval. A profit-making difference.

Does It Work?

An emphasis on listings and an "exclusive only" policy sounds great in theory. But does it work? Let me tell you a story.

We had an income office in trouble. It was three years old. There were over 100 active listings in the files but little or no business. A new manager was assigned. The first thing he did was review the existing inventory. He found that over fifty of the listings were opens. He cancelled all of them.

The office inventory was reduced to 57 properties. They were all exclusives. The inventory remained at that level for an entire year. During that time the office made a profit. In fact, it was the best year in the history of the office. In that year the office volume, with eleven men, came within $7,000 of the volume of another office with 27 men. The twenty-seven man office took a lot of "opens."

Another interesting thing happened during that year; many of the cancelled "opens" came back as exclusives and were sold. Of all listings taken, 38% were sold. This is a good record for income property. Those who work on "opens" are lucky to see 10% of their listings sold.

In that same office we found that an emphasis on "exclusives only" made the listing salesman do a better listing job. The result was that in all classes of income property, the relationship between listed price and sold price became very close. In apartment houses, for example, sales averaged 97.5% of the listed price. Apparently, when you fight for an exclusive you also get a better asking price.

One case illustrates this point. We had an industrial facility for sale. It was a 4½ acre battery manufacturing plant. Originally it had been listed as an "open" for $360,000. It didn't sell. About one year later we took it back as an exclusive. This time we fought for an "ex" and for a price. We got it at $220,000. It sold in four hours.

HOW TO GET AN EXCLUSIVE

To get an exclusive you must be able to convince the seller that an exclusive is the only way to get the job done. One of the best arguments for getting an exclusive is not an argument at all. It's an attitude. Some sales trainers call it the assumptive attitude. It's quite simple.

All you do is make up your mind to take nothing but exclusives.

Then, every listing call you go on, you assume you're going to take an "ex." Try it. You'll be amazed at how it works.

One of our salesmen recently made a call on an office building listing. After getting all of the necessary income and expense data he and the seller reached agreement on price and terms. So he filled out an exclusive listing and handed it to the seller for his approval. The seller wouldn't sign it.

"I thought you knew I never gave exclusives," he said. Our salesman was genuinely shocked. Such a thing had never entered his mind. "Open," indeed!

He explained the merits of an exclusive to the seller. No sale. So he left without a listing.

Two weeks later the seller called him—he got his exclusive.

Most sellers think many "opens" will get them more broker service than will one exclusive. You know better. But sellers don't really understand professional brokerage service. If you want an "ex" you'd better tell them about it.

Tell them about broker cooperation on exclusives. A good way to put this is to say, "I'd rather work on another broker's exclusive than on my own open." There is virtually no broker cooperation on "opens." At least no thoughtful, success-minded broker would ever reveal an uncontrolled piece of property to a fellow professional.

With an exclusive you can work with the trade. You can merchandise the property in an orderly manner to your fellow brokers. And you will. After all, the object of taking an exclusive is to make a sale. And it makes no difference to the professional broker, whether he sells it or whether it is sold by a fellow broker. Build your own cooperation story. It's a powerful exclusive listing tool.

Cream Puff Exclusives

Here's an idea that will get you exclusives on the most difficult type of property to list, the AAA, long-term tenant. Most of these properties are held by older owners. They have estate matters on their minds. They want to leave something for their families. Most of these owners know something about probate. With this background you have an ideal listing situation.

All you have to do is ask the owner, "Mr. Owner, have you ever considered making some moves now to simplify your estate? You own a prime piece of property. It will eventually pass into your estate. In some cases, such property has to be sold and it doesn't always bring as much as it would have, had you handled the sale during your lifetime. Perhaps it would be better to offer it now with you carrying back a first loan. This will maximize the price you get and give you a solid long-term loan. A first loan is a document of usually unquestioned value. There is little appraisal problem and the proceeds are easily divided among your heirs."

This presentation will often bring choice property onto the market with good (seller-carried) financing. This listing argument has produced over $25,000 in commission every year since we developed it. Put it in your own words and try it. It really works.

I Don't Want to Tie It Up

Many sellers give you the argument that they don't want to "tie up" their property on an exclusive. Here's a money-making answer to that old saw: "Mr. Seller, when your property is in the hands of an effective broker it isn't tied up. In fact, until you list it exclusively, and get a professional sales staff working on it, it is truly tied up." Then tell your company story.

Some sellers have just got to give it a go on their own before they will choose an exclusive agent. If you run into one of these do-it-yourselfers, you might try this: "Mr. Seller, the courtrooms are full of well-intentioned people who tried to handle this complicated process themselves." Then review with them some of the sophisticated legal problems involved in the sale of an income property. Most sellers aren't aware of them.

It Can Be Done

Getting an exclusive is a state of mind. It's just as easy to think exclusive as it is to think "opens." If you make up your mind to working only on exclusives, that's all you'll have. Of course, you'll have to turn down a lot of "opens" to maintain your exclusive policy while you're educating your clientele. But you won't lose anything. In fact, you'll save the centuries of time you formerly wasted on "opens."

To take exclusives you've got to be strong. You must not sacrifice a good long-run policy for the seeming short-term advantage of a good "open." There are no good "opens." You must believe this or you will never have an exclusive-only policy.

To get exclusives you've got to be good. You must know your craft. You must be better than the best that's around you. In short, you've got to know what you're talking about. To do this, you must make the investment in time and effort to really learn your business.

If you've never taken time out to learn your business, start doing it now, because without knowledge you've got very little to offer.

If you want exclusives, you must never take "opens." It's a small world. Word gets around fast. If you take any "opens" you'll be labelled an open listing broker. Once this happens, it takes time to repair the damage to your reputation and get on the "exclusive only" track again. Don't get off it in the first place; you'll save yourself a lot of time and trouble.

An exclusive inventory demands your exclusive attention. Reflect for a moment on the responsibility you accept when you take an exclusive. It is difficult to imagine a much greater expression of confidence in one person or firm on the part of another person than that which places a major property into one person's, or company's, hands on an exclusive basis. How then, if you take any exclusives, can you justify taking even one open? If you have an inventory of exclusives, you are breaching the faith put in you by those sellers if you ever show an open listing. All of your time, talent and energy ought to be spent on behalf of those who hired you on an exclusive basis.

The broker who continually courts the non-exclusive listing is following a course to economic disaster. He will not only bankrupt his business, he will bankrupt himself as a self-respecting human being. Certainly it's difficult to take only exclusive listings. But business failure is a lot more difficult to live with.

You may equivocate all you want to, but the fundamental truth remains. You can't get strong by acting weak. You can't build a solid image of yourself by constantly operating as a failure. Every time you take a non-exclusive listing, you have been weak. You have failed. You have chipped away at the foundation of your own self-respect and the cornerstone of your profession. If you do this often enough, your entire career will be undermined and will collapse.

Resolve to work only on exclusive listings. If you get nothing more than the determination to take only exclusive listings from this chapter, you will have gained a career.

Remember: Taking open listings is more than a waste of time— it is the waste of a career.

POINTS TO REMEMBER

—This is a listing business.
—Consistent sales volume comes from exclusive listings.

—Open listings lead to a closed business.

—The term of your listing should not be less than 180 days.

—Think about the difference between "shown" and "presented" as it applies to client registration.

—Buyers expect the property they are shown to be available for purchase. You must be able to deliver.

—Buyers are sick of the sloppy practices of open-listing brokers.

—An exclusive gives the broker time to get the best price.

—An exclusive simplifies negotiations.

—More sales fail for incomplete or inaccurate information than for any other reason.

—Exclusives show how serious and professional you are.

—Opens mean "I don't care about you."

—Without an exclusive a broker may be tempted to get on the buyer's side.

—Exclusives help sellers think straight.

—"Opens" lead to cut commissions.

—To get an exclusive assume you're going to get it.

—Most sellers don't understand professional brokerage service.

—Have a good broker cooperation story to tell.

—Property is "tied up" until an exclusive is entered into.

—Getting exclusives is a state of mind.

4

The Listing Process—Your Gold Mine

The greatest truth you will ever learn about income property is: This is a listing business. The second greatest truth is: *Listing is a process*. It is a process which you can constantly improve. There is no formula for instant listing success, but there is a program you can follow which will supply you with a sufficient number of saleable exclusive listings. That program is in this chapter.

THE SELLING SALESMAN

Before you can earn more dollars from your income property career, it is necessary that you know the truth about selling salesmen. There is no room for confusion on this point if you want long-term success.

The pure selling salesman doesn't take listings. It's a matter of pride with him to beat the odds. He is seldom a consistent performer. He may have a good year now and then, but his production is always erratic. He is constantly throwing the dice. Every day is a gamble. He lives in the hope that someone will take a good listing that he can "cream puff." He is a cherry-picker. In the long run, he fails. The good listing salesman will always out-perform him. The lister has a sure thing, he's got inventory.

Listers Are the Real Salesmen

It is a misnomer to call a non-lister a selling salesman. He's not a salesman at all; he's just an order taker. Top listers are the real selling salesmen.

It takes skill of the highest order to get good listings. The decision to buy is an easy one; there's an immediate, measurable benefit in a good purchase. It takes some salesmanship to bring about this decision, but it is of a far lower order than the salesmanship required to convince a seller to list exclusively. The immediate benefits to the seller, in agreeing to list, are not as apparent as are the benefits to the buyer when he agrees to buy.

If you enjoy practicing the art of selling, you'll be instantly attracted to the listing process; it's the real sales job in income property sales.

THE LISTING PROCESS

Fortunately, listing is a process; and it is a logical, orderly process. It is not a get-rich-quick scheme. It is not for the opportunist.

To be a good lister you must be career-minded. There are no fast and easy routes to quick listing production. Saleable listings are the result of long, hard, and careful work. They have their beginnings in the setting up of procedures for contacting property owners.

Your Address List

The first step to listing production is to build a list of property owners. There are many roads to the owner and you should explore them all. Success-program brokers have found, however, that the public records are the most efficient route.

Your local assessor maintains a role of real property owners. He keeps them in logical order. He identifies their holdings and he calculates an assessment on them. The assessor's information is valuable. Best of all, it's generally free. It's all the information you'll ever need for a good address list.

Assessor's Records Easy to Use

Good listers know their assessor's office from top to bottom. Some base all their listing efforts on information obtained from this source. If you are not totally familiar with your assessor's system you are facing a failure signal. Don't let this knowledge gap exist one more day. Get down to the assessor's office and ask one of the clerks to explain the system to you.

Pay special attention to how changes in ownership are recorded. Many men come away from the assessor's office with incomplete or inaccurate information simply because they don't know how to spot recent ownership changes. If you're using the assessor's records to build an ownership list, it is wasteful and expensive to direct letters or telephone calls to someone who no longer owns the property.

A Treasure House of Information

The assessor's office is a veritable treasure house to a lister. What are some of the things you can find there?

FIRST, sales. The location of all recent sales is generally pin-pointed in the assessor's records. It's great information and doubly valuable if you take the *next step* and look up the sales price.

THIRD, buyers. It's surprising how often the same owner's name crops up in any given area. If a name appears two or three times, make a note of it. When you get a listing, you've got a built-in buyer.

FOURTH, trouble. Quite often tax delinquencies are noted on your assessor's records. There could be real motivation to sell among this group of owners.

FIFTH, activity. Note all the sales. If there are very few owner-ship changes, you may be working a dead area. If there are many recent sales, it may be played out.

SIXTH, centers of influence. Ever notice how often several different owners have their tax bill sent to the same individual or firm? This observation could turn up an attorney with an active real estate practice; it could also lead you to a big property management company. Everytime you run across centers of influence, check them out —they will influence a good many listings.

We have just examined six valuable things you can dig up at the assessor's office. Keep all six in mind as you build your address list. Remember: Success-program brokers always try to get more than one use out of anything they do.

How to Contact Sellers

Planning and regularity of contact are the twin keys to listing success. To be a good lister you must be in regular contact, by mail, phone, or in person, with hundreds (yes, *hundreds*) of property owners.

Pick an area (really many areas) that you like. Set up a permanent record card for each property. Be sure to keep your records by property, not by owner. Ownerships change; property usually stays put. Give your record card some thought; do it right the first time. No one likes paperwork but when you're forced to do it (and it's absolutely essential here), it saves time to do it right and use it more than once.

Provide space on your record card for all the usual things. Be especially sure you have space to record every contact you've had with the current owner. Regularity of contact is one key to listing success. Contact each of your owners at least once every 90 days.

Your best possible contact is in person. The setting up of an in-person interview is the only purpose of any contact method. Until you see the owner face-to-face, you don't live for him; you are just a guy who sends him letters or calls him on the telephone. The seller must know you as an individual before he will list with you. He begins to know you when you first meet him in person.

Ten Ways to Meet the Owner

Here are ten time-tested success techniques for contacting your owners. These methods are part of the success-program of every good listing salesman. They'll produce listings for you.

1. Each time you get a listing, send all surrounding owners a recently listed letter.
2. Every time you make a sale, send each owner in the area a recently sold letter. You will find complete information on how to use the recently listed and recently sold letters in Chapter 6.
3. Send each owner a copy of their plat map, with their property outlined in red. Attach your business card. Better still, photograph your card as you copy the plat map on your office copier. The owner will keep the map, and your card will be a part of the picture. Enclose a short, handwritten note with the plat map asking the owner to call you when he wants to sell. You'll always get a lot of calls from this device, if only to thank you for the map.
4. Here's a real winner. Send each of your listing prospects a survey of recent sales in his area. Such information is fascinating news to an owner. Here's an example. It was printed on the company letterhead without any inside address. Even the salesman's signature was printed.

From the Desk of Dan Green,
Specialist in Apartment House Sales

Date	Units	Street	Listed Price	Selling Price	% of Listed Price
4/ 3/70	16 units	E. Elm	$165,000	$165,000	100%
4/ 4/10	3 units	on Walnut	21,000	21,000	100%
5/10/70	8 units	E. 15th	47,500	47,500	100%

From the Desk of Dan Green—Continued

6/15/70	10 units	N. Grove	80,000	75,000	93.7%
6/21/70	20 units	Hoover St.	149,900	142,000	94.7%
7/16/70	8 units	Park Pl.	85,000	85,000	100%
8/10/70	5 units	N. Grand	24,000	24,000	100%
9/ 5/70	14 units	S. Fox	130,000	127,500	98.1%
9/ 5/70	16 units	S. Fox	145,000	145,000	100%
11/10/70	20 units	E. Elm	147,500	137,500	93.2%
TOTALS			$994,900	$969,500	

Total Sales Prices Are 97.45% of Total Listed Prices.

The above are the APARTMENT BUILDINGS sold by the writer during the past year. There are 15 other full-time investment property salesmen in this office and the total office sales volume is many times the amount shown above.

Apartment houses are selling well if properly presented to the market by a professional organization. NOW is an excellent time to sell.

If you are thinking of selling, I would like to talk with you. I may be reached at 999-8600 or 997-2400.

Daniel Green

The above letter is an excellent example of a competent man at work. He lists from strength, not weakness.

5. Use your advertising. Send each listing prospect an example of your advertising. This is really powerful if you are using full-page ads. Accompany this mailing with a story stressing the heavy advertising done by your firm. Point out that this means you have MORE BUYER CONTACT.

6. Use your brochures. Send each prospect one of your company brochures. Always attach your card.

7. Advertise yourself. Reproduce all publicity about yourself and send it to your listing prospects. People like to do business with a man who is doing things.

8. Hold seminars. Use this topic: "How to Invest in Income Property and Make a Profit." Invite your listing clients. After two or three such seminars you'll be known as the leading income property specialist in your area.

9. Show them how to live without you. Create a booklet on "How to Sell Without a Broker." Send it to all of your for-sale-by-owners. After they've read how complicated and risky the whole process is, they'll call you to do the job for them.

10. Advertise! Advertise! Advertise—but not for listings! Dominate your area with "for sale" ads. You'll get more listings by accident than the non-advertising broker can get on purpose.

The building of a good owner file is the first step to a listing. Regular contact with these owners is your second step. Knowing how to handle a listing call is your third step—and it's the pay-off step.

THE LISTING CALL

Your contact method has turned up a seller who wants to talk with you. What do you do now? It's simple. You go make the call with a clear idea in your mind as to your method and your purpose.

One or Two Calls?

The method used in your listing call is the real art of listing. In this respect, home and income property listing may differ. In home listing the one-call method appears to be the most efficient and successful technique. In income property sales the two-call listing method appears to be best.

Income property sellers expect you to give serious attention to their sales problem. They want a thorough and thoughtful analysis of their property. Most of them refuse to believe much serious attention or thought can be expended in one call.

Your sales are large, the commissions are big. The sellers want lots of service for the thousands of dollars they pay you. Service begins at the point of listing. It is hard for the seller to get a strong impression of service in the one-call listing method. Many commission cuts start right here, with salesmen who shortcut the listing process.

The Two-Call Method

The two-call listing method may actually be many calls. The only thing you can be sure of is that it is more than one call. Here's how it works:

Your first step is to see the seller just as fast as you can. He's in the mood, he wants to talk. So get over there and talk to him. If possible, go by his property and refresh your memory of it before you keep your appointment with the seller. But if a visit to the property means a delay of more than an hour in seeing the seller, forget it. That's one of the strengths of the two-call method; you don't have to see the property first.

Your first call deals with you and your ability to serve the seller. It's a trading call. You tell the seller about yourself, he tells you about his property. Your purpose is to sell the company, sell yourself, sell the exclusive idea and get the facts on the property for sale.

It is vital that you use your first call to build a solid foundation under your relationship with the seller. You must distinguish yourself and your company from all others in the business. At the end of this call the seller must feel that you are the only one he wants to handle his sale. It's a long way between this listing call and a sale. But the sale is your goal. To get a sale you must have the seller's confidence. Start building it on your first call.

Telling Your Story

You must have a success story (I call it your company story) to tell about yourself and your company. How you put it together and how you tell it is up to you. It can be totally prepared and rehearsed and supported by visual aids, or it can be told almost incidentally. The "incidental" method is a good one, but it's difficult to use.

The idea of telling your company story "incidentally" is to drop in key points about yourself and your service as you discuss the seller's sales problems. The method presupposes a high degree of competency on your part. If you use it, you'll find it a powerful success technique. Here's an example:

You are in the seller's home. The interview has begun. The seller asks: "What do you think you could get for my property?" If you give him a price, you're dead. You don't have enough facts yet. A snap answer here will only irritate the seller and lessen his confidence in your professional ability. It may also lead to an argument over your opinion. (Ever have that happen?) You might try this answer: "It's our job to get top dollar for your property, Mr. Smith, and we're anxious to do that job. But, I am not in a position to say what that top-dollar price is right now. I don't have enough facts. Perhaps you'd be interested in seeing how my company goes about answering the price question."

Now, show him how you evaluate a property. This is part of your company story. Use an actual example from one of your recent sales. When you get through, you will have told the seller something of interest to him, and you'll have told part of your own story. Properly used, this technique can build a solid picture of competency.

The purpose of the first call is to sell yourself, your company, the exclusive, and to get the facts. Do it, and get out.

Typical First Call Problems

Price is always a problem. The one thing to avoid at all costs is stating your opinion of value before you know what the seller's opinion is. When the topic of price comes up, the main idea is to get the seller to commit himself on price first. His price gives you an insight into both his realism and his motivation. Most of the time the initial price will be too high, but knowing it defines the size of the problem. Here's another way to handle this situation:

From what you know of the area, the property is probably worth between $165,000 and $175,000. You ask: "What do you have to get for this property to accomplish your purpose in selling it, Mr. Roberts?" He answers (rather quickly): "I want $184,000 for it."

The problem now has a dimension. The seller's idea of price varies from yours in a range between $9,000 and $19,000. You can sink your teeth into this and set to work trying to narrow the difference. It's a job you'll do on the second call. His answer gives you a chance to tell a little more of your company story. In the first call you reply: "That's fine, Mr. Roberts. May I get the facts so I can evaluate your property and see if we can get that much for you?" Proceed to get all necessary details. Go slowly and work carefully. Insist on complete and accurate data. At this point you are using the price question to demonstrate how carefully you treat the sale of an investment property.

Actions speak louder than words; you'll never tell your company story better. Getting the facts is tough. But you must have them. The more you insist upon them, the more you demonstrate what a careful, thorough workman you are. Sellers often get nervous as you pursue the facts. If the seller complains at your insistence on complete and accurate information, you have a great opportunity. Tell him:

"Mr. Roberts, my object is not to take just another listing. My object is to get you a sale. Our experience has shown that more sales fall apart for lack of complete and accurate information than for any other reason." If he's motivated, he'll calm down.

Gathering the facts may be the biggest first-call problem. It is much better to get all the information during the listing process than it is to get it by bits and pieces as you work on the property.

Every time you call a seller during the term of your listing for some routine piece of missing information (like insurance coverage), you give him cause to think you are a sloppy, disorganized salesman. He also thinks, "My gosh! If he doesn't know that, no wonder he can't sell it!"

Facts Measure Motivation

There is another function of insisting upon full and accurate data from the seller. It is this: *The closer you get to the truth about the property the closer you get to the seller's motivation for selling.* Many sellers merely seek to test the market through a broker. Such sellers are not serious about selling. All they want is a market appraisal of their property. Such sellers scream the loudest when you press them for the facts. They had no idea it was going to be like this—Why, this takes time!

As you approach the truth, unmotivated sellers back off. Such sellers are easier to spot if you press for the facts. If they aren't motivated, don't take a listing. If all the owner wants is your opinion of the value of his property, give it to him. Leave him with a good feeling about you. You'll still be around when he really wants to sell.

How to Gather the Facts

There is one tool in your kit better suited than all others for gathering the facts. It is your listing form. It's the form best organized for the job. Think of it as a conditioning tool.

Get your listing form out in front of the seller on your first call. It's like showing an offer to purchase to a buyer early in the game. The more the client sees the forms you use, the less afraid of them he becomes. If the seller sees you working on your listing form now, he won't be scared to death when you get it out to take his listing.

Let's look at income as an example of how you gather facts. It is not enough to get the yearly gross income from the seller. The annual gross is merely the quantity of the income. The other aspect of income—quality—is quite important. For this reason you must have a breakdown of the income, tenant by tenant.

Consider a group of five stores. The annual gross income is $6,900. This is interesting but not too meaningful. Some obvious questions immediately leap into your mind: Are there leases? How long have the tenants been here? What about percentage clauses? You probe a little deeper. Three tenants pay $100 monthly, one pays $150, and the other pays $125. All occupy the same size space. Why the difference in rents? Is one over-rented? Have the others received concessions? These and all other questions must be answered; the answers affect your sale. You must know any property better than the owner does, if you expect to sell it. Dig for your facts.

Your first call comes to an end once you get all the facts you came for. *Get the facts and get out* is the rule. You need time to think and time to get acquainted with the property.

THE SECOND CALL

Go See It

Your first step in preparing for your second call is to visit the property. Your prelisting inspection procedure is the same as the pre-showing inspection described in Chapter 10. This similarity of procedure may explain why so many sales are made by the men who take the listing. Do your inspection job well and return to your office.

Evaluate the Property

As a professional real estate man you are familiar with several valuation procedures. All of them have their proper use. Your listing client, however, is not generally familiar with the many valuation techniques. He is, for example, only confused by talk about reproduction cost. Further, he has little confidence in something he does not understand. He will argue with you over comparable sales. They're so seldom really comparable.

Most sellers do understand income and expense. After all, they've been collecting the income and paying the bills for some time. Rent and expense are real to them. For this reason, you should use the income approach to value in evaluating most properties.

The income approach to value puts you on common ground with your seller. It is the most useful approach for this reason and, except in rare cases, an income property is worth the capitalized value of the income it produces.

Some Tips on Using Your Evaluation

Your second step in preparing for your second call is to prepare an income approach to value analysis. This analysis will show a true net income. Here's what you do with that figure:

Capitalize it at three cap rates. The use of three capitalization rates sets up discussion possibilities. The use of one rate causes arguments with the seller. Let's look at an example of the rates in use.

After establishing the income and deducting all expenses plus an allowance for vacany and maintenance you've established a net income of $8,400 per year. Now select three cap rates. The rates you use are:

1. The rate you feel is correct for your area.

2. ½ point below this rate.

3. ½ point above this rate.

If 10% is the current rate, use 9½%, 10% and 10½%. You are now prepared to say to your seller:

"You've agreed that the net income on this property is $8,400 per year. Let's see what different buyers might be willing to pay for this income. If the buyer wanted a 9½% return, he'd pay about $88,421, if he wants 10% he'd pay $84,000, and if he required 10½% on his money the price would be $80,000. It appears that the value is between $80,000 and $88,500. Our experience indicates that you should be able to get about $84,000 for this property."

The use of three cap rates creates a reasonable range of value. It allows you to select the one in the middle (a logical compromise) as your suggested price. The procedure maximizes the seller's price if your capitalization rate is correct and if you have all the income and all the expenses.

Three-Column Analysis

Before you make your second call, set all your evaluation data down on paper. Here's a proven success technique:

Do a three-column analysis of the property. In column one use the seller's price, in column two use your idea of market value. Label the third column "difference." Use column three to show the mathematical difference between column 1 and column 2. The third column then becomes a measure of the degree of difficulty the seller faces in finding a buyer. A partial example appears below:

	Column 1	Column 2	Difference
Price	$184,000	$170,000	$14,000
Loans	$145,000	$155,000	$10,000
Down payment	$ 39,000	$ 15,000	$24,000

(Continue with the balance of the analysis showing all items such as income, expense, net income, spendable.)

With this kind of a spread sheet, you are prepared to focus on the problem. In reviewing it with the seller you might say something like this: "Mr. Jones, we appear to be about $14,000 away from what our experience indicates is a market price. This might not be too much of a hindrance to a sale, but when you consider we are also asking $24,000 more in down payment than is normal, I feel we are going to have some real trouble getting you your price." This will usually give you all the opening you need for a friendly discussion as to how you and the seller can put together a saleable package.

Purpose of Second Call

The second call has two purposes. The first is to get the right price, the second is to get the listing. In all listing situations, there are two sales to make. You must first sell yourself and your company so the owner will want to list with you exclusively. Your second sale is to convince the owner to list at a market price. Success-program salesmen never try to fight the exclusive battle and the price battle in the same call. By using the two-call method, you fight the exclusive battle first. This saves time. If you don't win the exclusive battle, you don't have to make the second call.

CONTROLLING FEAR

Many second calls fall apart because the seller and the salesman seem to be at war. The salesman knows the price is going to be too high or the terms ridiculous. Or the seller will only want to list for 90 days. The seller knows the salesman is just there to tie his property up, hoping to grab a quick commission. (He's trying to steal it.) Or he's going to be asked to sign a 180-day listing at too low a price. In short, there is fear and suspicion in the mind of each party. Such a situation should not exist. When it does, it is your fault. It is your job to control fear, both yours and the seller's. And you can do it.

Believe In Yourself

To control fear you must have strong convictions about the value of yourself and your services. You must believe, without reservation, that most real estate transactions would never be made without the service of a dedicated broker. You must expect that this call will be successful. It will be. All calls are successful. You never lose.

Nothing transmits quicker than how weak or strong you feel. If there is the least sign of uncertainty, weakness, fear, or lack of conviction in you, the seller will sense it immediately. To be a listing salesman you must be strong. You must believe in first-class brokerage service and your ability to render it.

Here's the best trick you'll ever learn to control seller fear: *Be on the seller's side!* Serious sellers want to hire someone who can help them.

Don't Argue

Never argue with the seller over his price. Don't let the situation develop to where it is his price against your price. You don't have a price. You have an opinion of how the marketplace will value the property. Here's what to say to avoid all price arguments: "Considering the market conditions we are facing today, it looks like buyers will value this property between $165,000 and $175,000. The price you pick is up to you, Mr. Doe. The closer your price is to $165,000 the faster it will sell. If you're in no hurry to find a buyer, then a price closer to $175,000 is the one to choose. The higher price will allow us (you and the seller) to test the market for 30 days. If we get no favorable response in this time, I'll come and see you and we can review our pricing policy."

By using this dialogue you demonstrate that you are working with the seller to get him a prompt sale at a top price. The use of a range of value also marks you as a careful man.

Getting the Signature

The moment of truth arrives in every listing call. You've eventually got to ask the seller to sign the listing. It's a critical point; your sales job may be just starting. Once the seller signs that listing, he has hired you, and there's no turning back. It's a real crisis point for many sellers. Here's how to get it signed:

STEP ONE—Don't rush.

Take your time as you fill out the form. Be calm, take it slow and easy. Nothing shakes a seller's confidence more than a man in a hurry.

STEP TWO—Discuss everything.

Verify each point as you enter it on your listing. Especially down payment, terms of secondary financing or any special contingencies.

STEP THREE—Hand it to him.

Say: "Please approve this right here and we'll get to work selling your property."

STEP FOUR—Shut up.

Sit back and say no more—it's his move. He'll sign it or object, either way you win. If he objects you will answer the objection and invite his approval again. If he signs it, you move to the next step, which is:

STEP FIVE—Get out of there!

There is much left to do but the sooner you leave the better. It's been a long, hard struggle for both of you. Take the pressure off— go home.

CONDITIONING THE SELLER

At some point in your listing process you will have to condition the seller to the many minor problems that may crop up while you are trying to sell his property. Whether this conditioning should be done at the end of the second call or at another time is an unsettled point. Every professional agrees that it is a job that has to be done during the listing process.

These are the things that you must discuss with your seller:

1. other broker activity
2. quick offers
3. low offers
4. showing without an appointment
5. office caravan
6. buyers without the broker
7. closing details
8. advertising
9. talking to buyers during a showing
10. resident manager cooperation

Go over each of these points; if you don't, you're buying trouble.

Offer Problems

If you've taken the listing near the top of the price range, you may be in for some offer problems. Condition the seller to treat all offers seriously. There are two things to keep in mind:

1. You may be the one who gets a low offer, and
2. A low offer is better than no offer.

Generally speaking, the better the listing the better the offer. When you're trying to sell, however, there is no such thing as a bad offer.

Explain how counter-offers are made. Tell the seller you expect him to make a written counter-offer should he receive an offer that doesn't quite meet his needs. If you condition the seller to the correct procedure, you won't run into the problem of torn-up offers or stalled negotiations.

Don't forget to mention fast offers. If you avoid this area you may find the seller unwilling to accept an as-listed offer if he gets it too quickly. One way of handling the possibility of a fast offer is to say: "We have a backlog of buyers, this may be just the thing one of them is looking for. If it is, you may receive an offer rather quickly. We find that most listings either sell early in the listing or late. If one of our present buyers does not buy your property, it will take time to find Mr. *Right*."

ADVERTISING

Most sellers expect you to advertise. Explain your policy in this regard. Try to avoid a definite advertising commitment or schedule. An easy way of handling this problem is to tell the seller you will be reviewing your sales effort with him in 30 days and if he is dissatisfied with the advertising (or anything else) you'll discuss it and take action at that time.

Listing is the key to your success. It is not a get-rich-quick scheme. You must go about it in an orderly, logical way. Build an ownership file and contact your owners regularly. Practice listing every chance you get until you are an expert on the listing process—it's your gold mine!

POINTS TO REMEMBER

—Listing is a process.
—You can learn to be a better lister.
—Top listers are the real selling salesmen.
—Set up several listing areas.
—Be in regular contact with hundreds of owners.
—Know the assessor's office.
—Keep permanent listing records.
—Use at least 10 ways of prospecting for listings.
—Use the two-call listing method.
—On your first call, sell yourself, sell your company, sell the exclusive.
—On your second call, sell your price, take the listing.
—Learn how to handle the price problem. Never argue.
—Condition the seller.

5

How to List Property
at the Right Price

The real estate profession has a big alumni; we are literally surrounded by our graduates. Unfortunately, most graduates did not leave the business because they succeeded; most of them left as failures. They can prove through hard-won personal experience that this is not a listing business. Many of them took lots of exclusive listings, yet they failed. They failed because they forgot (or never learned) that the object of taking a listing is to make a sale. To get sales, you must take *saleable* listings. To take saleable listings you must have the right attitude, superior knowledge, outstanding sales ability, understanding toward the seller, and know how to speak in terms of his self-interest.

YOUR ATTITUDE

The failure and the inexperienced man have one thing in common —They know, with all their heart, that this is a negotiating business. Both depend upon buyers to do their listing job for them by making an offer. The success-program salesmen know this is a negotiating business too. The difference between success and failure is often not what you do, but how and when you do it.

The successful salesman expects to be constantly negotiating price. During the listing process he works with his seller. During the sales process he negotiates with the buyer to get him to pay the fair listed price.

Work with the Odds

Most ordinary brokers are too weak to fight the price battle with anyone, especially with the seller. The attitude that an offer cures everything (He'll sell it, just bring him an offer.) is so deeply ingrained that it is unthinkable to really get into the price question before an offer is in hand. To be blunt, most such men won't do their best until there is money (an offer) on the table.

Waiting for an offer to soften up the seller leads to failure more times than it does to success. Weak listing salesmen are weak selling salesmen. As such they sell 10%, or less, of their listings. Typically they will receive offers on about 20% of their listings. They have, therefore, only one chance in five of ever discussing price with their seller. Success-program salesmen have a 100% chance of discussing price because they always fight the price battle on their second listing call. And, they fight as honest men without the buyer's check in front of them.

Make a Trade

Here's a trade for you. Like most two-way trades it's going to be tough to make. It may be the most difficult exchange you're ever involved in. It requires you to trade one attitude for another. It's a trade you have to make if you want to get on the success program and stay on it. Here it is:

Trade the "let's get it listed and get an offer idea" for "let's get the property listed *right* in the first place."

You Never Lose

It is disappointing to fully prepare for a listing call, execute it well, and come away without the listing. But you must be prepared for, and be able to cope with, such disappointment if you want to get the property at the right price.

Here's an example: Recently I went to list a small vacant lot. It was 10,580 square feet and was suitable for building a four-unit apartment building. Its market value was $10,000 to $12,000. The price was established after two to three hours work researching comparable sales, plus a reproduction cost analysis. (We built a mythical building on it.) A check of the public records showed the current owner bought the lot eight months previously for $12,000, with $2,400 down to an interest-only first loan of $9,600.

The seller was shown the price evidence. He agreed with the evaluation of $10,000 to $12,000. He wanted to list for $14,000. Here's part of the conversation: "Mr. Smith, if you list at $14,000 and a serious buyer offers you $12,000 cash, what will you do?"

"I'd turn it down."

"Do you think it would be good business to involve your time, my time and the time of the buyer in a hopeless enterprise?"

He didn't, and I left without a listing. But I did not leave empty handed, for I had his respect and good will. The property was later listed at $12,000 and sold within a week.

You never lose by walking out on a poor listing. You gain the time you might have wasted on it and you gain the seller's respect for you as a man who knows his business and who means business.

YOUR KNOWLEDGE

In Chapter 8 I will review some aspects of the price problem as it relates to the use of the common evaluation techniques. In this section we look at a few ideas on how to use your information.

It is not the purpose of this chapter to show you how to evaluate property. You already know that. Our purpose is to discover new and effective ways of putting what you know to work.

Using Comparable Sales

Comparable sales can be useful in price discussion *if* they are really comparable sales. The twin problems of comparable sale data are: Accuracy and Suitability.

Your data must be accurate to be believable. This means an extensive use of the public records, to establish sales prices, and careful record keeping on your own sales. Resolve never to present comparable sales data to a client unless you are sure of two things: (1) The client could verify it independently if he wanted to, and (2) you'd present exactly the same data if you were testifying under oath.

The need for suitability can't be overstressed. Too many salesmen try to force all similar properties into the same pattern and then sell the idea that such groupings are comparable. They seldom are. When your owner feels your so-called comparables aren't really comparable, you might as well give up, because confidence in you has been lost. Don't make the error of believing, for example, that all ten units are alike and, therefore, any ten-unit apartment you try to list may be compared to all ten units you've ever listed. Such an idea won't sell to an owner because it isn't true.

Here's an example of using comparable sales to get the price you want. It is a strong story because it has truth and statistical logic in it.

The listing client owns a four-unit building. It is on a street of 17, four-unit buildings, all built at the same time by the same builder. Exterior elevations are all different but the interiors are identical on all 17 properties. They all sold three years ago for $54,000 with $4,000 down.

A search of the records reveals four sales in the last 14 months. There is one current offering. The recent sales are:

#1 $57,000—$5,700 down
#2 $59,500—$8,500 down
#3 $59,500—$6,000 down
#4 $62,500—$7,000 down

The current listing is at $60,500 with 10% down.

You are talking with an owner who wants to know at what price he should list. You might show him the recent sales history in the area (Be sure to indicate the address of each property plus both buyer's and seller's names.) and explain it like this:

"You will notice, Mr. Ellis, that the price for these identical buildings ranges from $57,000 to $62,500. The current competition is $60,500. Why don't we disregard the lowest and the highest price. They appear to be exceptions to the pattern. That leaves two sales at $59,500 and one current listing at $60,500. It would seem that your best approach to the market would be $59,500 with a 10% down payment. How do you feel about it?"

The seller will, of course, reply, and further discussion will follow. In the typical case you and your data will control the direction of the discussion.

Many brokers make comparables live for the seller by using three sets of data:

recent sales,
current listings,
expired listings.

They explain that each of these categories may be thought of in a meaningful way. This is the way:

Recent sales = the price buyers *paid*.

Current listings = the price buyers *can pay*.

Expired listings = the price buyer's *wouldn't pay*. `

Paid, can pay and *wouldn't pay*—such terms have power; they make the idea come alive.

USING THE INCOME APPROACH

We have already seen, in Chapter 4, the great strength of the income approach to value. Sellers understand and accept it. You and the seller are on common ground when you use it.

Derived Data

In the normal income approach presentation you list the price, loans, down payment, income, expense, loan payments, cash spendable and other pertinent data. Quite often that's as far as it goes. There are, however, some interesting and useful relationships between the data which you can use to help you get the right price. These relationships are so common they've come to be called rules of thumb.

The Gross Multiplier

Times gross (or gross multiplier) is one of these. It really has limited usefulness due to the almost impossible requirement that the properties and nature of income be truly comparable. Yet the times gross figure is highly acceptable to both buyers and sellers as an indication of value. It is generally used in connection with apartment houses and motels and can range between 4 times and 10 times. You should, of course, develop typical multipliers for your own area. But, more important, think the multiplier idea through and come to an understanding of it. It's surprising how often you can increase your professional stature in the eyes of your seller by a brief discussion of what the multiplier means. If you're going to use it, use it as you would comparable sales data.

Percentages

After you've finished your income approach to value analysis, calculate some common percentage relationships and compare them to the standard relationships in your area. Here's an example:

Item	Subject Property	Standard for Area
Expenses as % gross income	48%	35–50%
Loan payments as % of gross income	52%	40–50%
Cash spendable	0	10–25%
Down payments as % of sales price	5%	10–20%

Such an analysis will often dramatically highlight the problems with the potential listing. It lets you discuss the differences between the potential listing and the standard for the area. Some sellers respond to a percentage figure better than they do to the actual dollar figure. Try this idea, it too can make the figures live for a seller.

Be Accurate

Don't attempt to use figures to help your seller see his true position unless you have a reliable calculator. It's a disaster to have the client discover simple, mathematical errors. Such errors lead the seller to believe you are deliberately trying to deceive him or that you are careless. Either way, you lose. Mathematical errors are a controllable factor. Control them. Check everything twice, discover all mistakes before you leave the office.

TALKING PRICE TO YOUR SELLER

The emphasis in this chapter, as it is throughout the book, is on the need for thorough preparation and planning. The hard work you do *before* you make a call is a great personal motivator. The more work you do before the call, the more anxious you will be to make it. Preparation and planning pay off in a more vital and dynamic presentation.

The Seller's Self-interest

There is no one in the world more important to the seller than himself. The great danger of working with facts and figures is that you might forget to present them in terms of the seller's self-interest.

The Second Mortgage

Consider the problem of good secondary financing as it relates to price. The economics of real estate dictate that most overpriced properties have big second loans. To put it another way: To get more than a property is worth, you have to offer it with a low down and a big second. Such overpriced sales can work against the self-interest of the seller. Look at these figures.

Normal		*Overpriced*
100,000	Price	110,000
15,000	Down	11,000
70,000	First loan	70,000
15,000	Second loan	29,000

The fair price is $100,000. You know it. The seller knows it. The first loan lender will also know it. Properly appraised, the property will not attract a bigger first loan just because the sales price goes up. When the price gets too high, the down payment must come down. The seller-carried loan must take up the slack. It carries *all* the speculative risk in the transaction.

In many states the seller's only practical recourse in the event of default on his second loan is to foreclose and recover his property. If the seller's only security is the property, he's got to be foolish to take advantage of any buyer and thus set up the chance of a foreclosure. The expense of foreclosure, plus the loss through a disappointed buyer's neglect of a poor investment, is often greater than the cash the seller got from a sale.

When secondary financing is involved you've got a great chance for getting the right price. You might say it like this:

"Mr. Jones, I'm sure that when you make this sale you want to keep it sold, don't you? What I mean by that is this—you don't want to take the property back in a year or two, do you? If your object is to sell it and keep it sold, you've got to make a sale that is fair to you and gives the new owner a chance of making it. It is against your best interest to sell at too high a figure with too low a down payment. Such a sale burdens the property with too much debt. If the excessive debt causes the new owner to lose money, he will walk away from the property. But first he will try to take his revenge on you by getting back as much of his investment as he can before you can act to recover the property. Typically, such a disappointed buyer waits until tax time, fails to pay them and thus recovers something. He will also miss one or two payments and neglect all maintenance in his desperate attempt to cut his losses. The result is often that you take back a run down property burdened by unpaid taxes, several back payments, and many vacancies. All this can be avoided by selling at the right price."

It Can Backfire

Such a presentation can backfire. Some sellers immediately respond with: "If seconds are so bad I won't carry one!"

Now you've got him. Your response is: "That's fine, Mr. Jones. Let's see what the price is for cash."

The cash price is, of course, much lower; and when the seller sees this he generally ends up listing at a fair price with a normal second. You won't get a cash-to-the-loan listing one time in fifty calls, if you use this approach. When you do get a cash price, you still win because good property, priced right, always sells.

The "You Get" Approach

In the last analysis the price or the down payment are of incidental importance to a seller. Most people have one overriding, all-consuming interest. It is this: How much do I get out of it? The amount they get (after costs) is generally compared to the amount they put into the investment. It's easy to spot such sellers; they're the honest ones. They state, "I want (so much) *net to me.*"

"Net to me."—those are money words. You will never take a net listing, of course, but when you hear those words, move in with your "you get" presentation. Show the seller exactly what he gets out of the sale. Work it out in front of him on paper. Head up the paper with "YOU GET." Make two columns. The first column is cash in, the second is cash out. Here's an example:

YOU GET

	Cash In		Cash Out
Down payment	$20,000	Expenses:	
Second loan	20,000	Commission	$6,000
		Closing costs	150
		Title insurance	285
		Building inspection	100
		Miscellaneous	100
Total	$40,000		$6,635

$40,000 − $6,635 = $33,365 APPROXIMATELY
You get: $13,365 cash + $20,000 7-year second paying 7% at $200 monthly

Here are some money-making tips on using this idea:

First, figure it out in front of the seller. Don't prepare it ahead of time.

Second, always combine the cash and the second mortgage. Treat the total as cash. It doesn't make sense to do this, but it works.

Third, always write down "approximately" in large letters.

Fourth, stress the monthly income and the interest on the second.

"You get" will make you money. It's a good listing technique; it's an even better technique for getting an offer accepted.

I Paid More Than That for It!

There is no time when careful research pays bigger dividends than when you hear "I paid more for it than that!" The unfortunate truth is that most often such a statement is not true. True or not, it helps your case.

A deliberate lie on the seller's part indicates you haven't yet gained his confidence. Such a statement means you must go back to your first-call procedure and sell him on yourself and your company. You might also be facing an unmotivated seller. Anyone who wants to sell levels with you. When motivation is lacking, either get it listed at the right price or forget it.

Some sellers are lying to themselves. Quite often a seller will add all payments and expenses to his purchase price and convince himself that he has more in the property than he actually has. For some reason they never deduct the income received. An equity build-up analysis will usually be the answer in this case.

When a seller is truly selling for less than he paid, you can soften the blow in several ways. You must, at all costs, avoid stating that he made a mistake in ever buying the property. Try this:

"Mr. Dokes, I'm sure that at the time you bought this *you did the right thing*. No one can foretell the future. As it turned out, conditions have changed. We must do as you did when you bought it— face the facts as they are today."

Never call the seller a liar, even if you know he is. It does no good to win the battle and lose the war.

Here's another answer to "I paid more for it than that." You say: "Granted, Mr. Dokes. Let me ask you this: Does that fact really change anything about the current market value of this property? Would it be worth less, for example, if you had gotten it as a gift?"

POINTS TO REMEMBER

—The object of taking a listing is to make a sale.

—Negotiate the price during the listing process; sell the price during the selling process.

—Waiting for an offer to do your listing job leads to failure more times than it does to success.

—You never lose by refusing a poor listing.

—Comparable sales data must be both accurate and suitable.

—Calculate the percentage relationships between significant items on your income approach to value analysis.

—Research your sales and establish common percentage relationships from the actual experience in your area.

—Be accurate. Double-check all figures.

—Speak to the seller's self-interest.

—Use the "You Get" approach.

—The price the seller paid is not an indication of value; it may indicate motivation to sell.

6

Profit-Making Letters

One of your basic problems will always be how to get more exposure to people who want to sell. The more sellers you talk to, the more money you'll make. The success-program salesman knows this. The more times you get your name and your body before people who want to sell, the greater your chance for success.

In this chapter you will find three profit-making listing letters. They are great exposure getters. All of them have been in use for years—they are field-tested, they get results. Two of these letters get fantastic results. The third is a good performer too, but seldom yields listings in the same amount as the first two.

THE ROLE OF LETTERS

As you read this chapter, please keep this in mind: The only purpose of any of these letters (regardless of what they seem to say) is to help you get listings.

As a real estate salesman your first job is finding people who want your services. In this respect all salesmen have something in common. Whether you sell washing machines or real estate, you have to dig up prospects.

As an income property salesman, you have a problem not shared by salesmen in most other fields. You are unique. You must make a sale in order to be in position to make a sale. You have to convince a seller to list with you before you can talk to any buyer. You have two prospecting jobs: looking for sellers and looking for buyers. Prospecting for sellers is your most important job. Good letters can do a big part of that job for you.

Letters Get It Started

Letters are a convenient prospecting device; they get you started. A good listing letter program is not a substitute for action, it is a way of organizing yourself for action. Never let your letters turn you into a chairbound salesman. Your letter program ought to be used to get you out in the field talking to buyers and sellers.

The Job of a Letter

The main job of a listing letter is to get a reply from someone who wants to sell. If a letter gets a response, the letter's job is done and your job begins.

Your job is to get an appointment. It's that simple. You send a letter. You get a reply. You make an appointment to see the seller. It is then up to you to convince the owner to list with you.

Don't Be Confused

Don't be confused about a letter program. You may send out fifty letters and get ten replies. If you make five appointments to see sellers and get no listings, it is not the fault of your letter program. The program did its job—it got you ten replies. The only role of a listing letter is to get a reply. Good letters get replies, good salesmen get listings.

THREE LETTERS

Here are three questions that will make you money. If you ask them of everyone you meet, you may never have the time or the need to send out listing letters.

1. Do you want to sell any income property?
2. Do you want to buy any income property?
3. Do you know anyone who wants to buy or sell income property? These are also the only three questions you try to ask by mail.

Recently Listed Letter

This letter asks two questions:
1. Do you want to buy?
2. Do you want to sell?

Mr. Robert Smith
123 Elm Street
    City,   State

NEWS ABOUT YOUR NEIGHBORHOOD

We have a good property for sale near you.

If you are interested in another investment in this area please call me.

Should you wish to sell your property, we are in an excellent position to merchandise it for you now while we are actively showing our current offering.

I may be reached at 220-7711.

Frank Powell

This letter is step one in a two-step program. It works with a Recently Sold letter to be discussed later.

Putting it to Work

The Recently Listed letter is sent to all owners surrounding a new listing. Hopefully, this letter will soon be followed by your Recently Sold letter. The mechanical steps are:

FIRST, have a supply of the letter (letterhead and body copy only) printed.

SECOND, prepare a list of the names and addresses of the surrounding property owners.

THIRD, give your address list and a supply of the letters to your typist.

FOURTH, keep your address list, it will be used again when you sell the property.

Your Address List

The names and addresses for this program may usually be obtained at your assessor's office. To make the time and effort spent in gathering these addresses pay, set up your list so you can use it more than once.

An obvious second use for this list is in sending out Recently Sold letters. It may also be used for mailing other forms of advertising. Success-program salesmen multiply their chances for success by always trying to get more than one use out of anything they do.

Recently Sold Letters

This is the letter everyone likes to send. And, judging by the replies, it's the one surrounding property owners like to receive. A 20% response is not an unusual performance for this letter. Here it is:

> Mr. Robert Smith
> 123 Elm Street
>   City,   State
> Re: 125 Elm Street
>
> We have recently sold the above mentioned property in your neighborhood. If you have owned your property for three or more years, you might consider disposing of it now. It is often possible, by sale or trade, to secure important tax advantages and an improvement in your income.
>
> Buyers with substantial means contact our office each day. As a result, a large percentage of our exclusive listings sell in a very short time with a highly profitable return to the seller.
>
> Our staff of over 100 full-time sales representatives is thoroughly trained to serve your real estate needs. The enclosed brochure illustrates the inside story that has enabled our company to become one of (your state's) largest real estate organizations.
> I may be reached at 999-8100.
>
> *Robert Anderson*

How the Recently-Sold and Listed Letters Are Used

The Recently Sold letter is sent to all owners surrounding a recent sale. As mentioned earlier, the ideal situation is to have this letter go out not long after these same owners receive your Recently Listed letter. It's a real one-two punch. After a couple of Recently Listed and Recently Sold letters from you, these owners will think you're the only real estate man left on earth.

How They Work

Here's an example of how these letters work:
Recently we took a listing on a deluxe (real pride-of-ownership) four unit. There were 17 other deluxe fours on the street. All 17 received the Recently Listed letter. Two or three owners called, but none of them were interested in buying our listings and we got no more listings. One of them sold. We sent out 17 Recently Sold letters.

Four owners called, three listings were taken. One more sale was made.

In another case, a two-block area, we took every listing and made every sale for two years. Such results are not unusual. I have seen the chain go unbroken for three years, with a listing followed by a sale followed by more listings and more sales.

General Listing Letter

This is the least successful of all listing letters. It is included here because you need something to get you started in areas where you have no listings and, consequently, no sales. The number of replies generated by this letter seldom exceeds 5%. Here's an example:

Mr. Robert Smith
123 Elm Street
      City,   State
Re: Your Property at 123 Elm Street

In passing your property today, it appeared to be of the type that many of our buyers have been asking for. I would like to know if you are interested in selling this property.

If you have owned your property for three or more years, it may be to your advantage to sell or trade now. Your equity in a larger property might easily provide you with more income and some important tax advantages. I'll be glad to discuss with you how you might improve your position.

Please call me if you have any questions. I may be reached at 210-3303.

Randolph Smith

How It's Used

This letter is sent into virgin territory. You have no history there. You're looking for listings so you can start your Recently Listed, Recently Sold sequence. You are a stranger in the area. You have no signs out, you have no results to talk about. You must, therefore, work very carefully. It will not be enough to just compile a list of names and send out some letters. You will have to spend time in the neighborhood and get familiar with all the property there. Unless you know the area, you won't be able to turn a reply into an appointment.

Handling a Reply

When a seller calls in response to this General Listing letter, you've got to be good to get your appointment. One way to increase your reply-appointment ratio is to mark on your area map, or on your address list, some outstanding characteristic of each property.

Make note of things like: building color, landscaping, pool or no pool, open or closed garages, number of stories. Then, when the seller calls, you can say something like this: "Oh yes, Mr. Smith. Yours is the yellow stucco building with the pool in the courtyard, isn't it?" Such a remark shows the seller you have more than a casual interest in his property.

Personal Follow-Up

The General Listing letter is weak. Because of this you must pay special attention to your follow-up procedure. It's always a good idea to follow-up this letter with a telephone call. Your call will increase the impact of your program. Keep the General Listing letter in mind as you read the following success techniques.

SUCCESS TECHNIQUES

There are a few things you must pay particular attention to if you wish to profit most from a letter program. Things like the appearance of your letter, its general quality, the timing of your mailings, and your follow-up.

Quality Pays

It is necessary, because of the numbers involved, to use a form letter in your listing letter program. But it doesn't have to look like a form letter. Your letters can have a custom, individually-typed look if you follow a few tested rules.

First, don't skimp anywhere. Use good paper and a matching envelope of never less than 25% rag content.

Second, pay for a first-class printing job.

Third, make sure every letter that goes out is perfect. Don't try to save on typing costs. If it costs you ten cents each to get your letters typed, it is cheap if the work is perfect. Sign each letter yourself and, if it isn't right, don't send it.

Custom Look

The more "custom" your letter looks, the more effective it will be. To get that custom look have the body copy typed on the same typewriter that is going to be used in preparing the mailings. Then have your letter printed by offset. Work with your printer; he'll show you how to do it.

Use a carbon ribbon in your typewriter when typing the inside address and the close. These ribbons give a very black impression. Most readers can't detect any difference between the typed and printed portions of the letter when a carbon ribbon is used. If you do enough of this kind of mailing, you ought to consider using automatic, programmed typewriters. Then all your letters will have a custom look.

Letter Style

The three example letters are set up in the block style. This is deliberate. The block style is clean and modern. The use of this style implies that yours is a clean and modern operation.

In the block style everything lines up on the left margin. This makes it easier for your typist and less expensive for you. You will also note that both the salutation and complimentary close are eliminated; it saves time and money.

The block style may seem strange if you've never seen it. In years of using it, however, I've never heard anyone complain about the general layout of the letter or the missing "Dear Sir" or "Truly Yours."

Timing

Listing letters should be mailed with two things in mind:
1. the convenience of the reader,
2. your convenience.
It is generally a poor idea to mail them so that they arrive on a Friday or a Saturday. Most people will either set them aside until the beginning of the week (and thus lose them) or will call at once. An immediate call may result in an appointment time inconvenient to you. Letters received on Saturday generally require an immediate in-person call. This creates some scheduling jam-ups; whereas letters received on Tuesdays or Wednesdays generally permit you to sched-

ule an appointment far enough ahead to avoid conflict with your other appointments.

You might also consider the competition your letter faces when it arrives on a Saturday. Your customer is usually interested in his own week-end activities; hence your business mail gets little attention.

Follow-up

If you send out hundreds of letters each week and just sit back waiting for phone calls, you're not going to get the kind of results you want. Your follow-up is the key to the success of your program.

Most users of the program keep a schedule. They know when each batch of letters should be received. Let us say you send out twenty letters on Monday. They should all be received by Wednesday. Give the prospect a day or two to call you. For or five of them will. Then Thursday night or Firday night call all the rest of them.

Here is what you say: "This is Dan Green of Red Carpet Realty. I sent you a letter this week." Now PAUSE. If the prospect replies: "Oh, yes, Mr. Green I just finished reading it," you can generally tell by his voice if there is any interest and you can go on with the conversation.

If, on the other hand, the prospect says: "Dan, who?" You can assume little interest in selling. The pause is a quick qualifying device.

Copy Comments

If your copy is right, you can count on some phenomenal results. The example letters regularly pull a 5–20% return. To anyone familiar with direct mail campaigns, such results are truly amazing.

Your letter must contain news. Not the kind of news you read in your daily paper but news of vital interest to the seller, news about his property. That's the reason the Recently Listed letter features the headline:

NEWS ABOUT YOUR NEIGHBORHOOD

The Recently Sold letter contains the most interesting news of all to someone thinking of selling—something sold!

Your copy must be definite. It must deal with a particular property and it must be true. These letters get superior readership because they are believable.

Use of Addresses

For proper results you must handle the address problem skillfully. You will notice that the Recently Sold letter refers to the property just sold by its address. No address is given in Recently Listed letter. There are two reasons for this. First, you do not wish to tempt either buyer or seller into direct negotiation. Secondly, you want to control other broker activity.

If you put the address on your Recently Listed letter, you may find some adjoining owner going to his own broker to buy it. You may then find yourself cooperating with an unskilled broker. That's not why you sent the letter.

POINTS TO REMEMBER

—Letters are not a substitute for action, they are a way of organizing for action.

—The job of a listing letter is to get a reply.

—Letters get replies, only you can get a listing.

—To turn replies into appointments makes notes about the area and use the information in your notes when the seller calls.

—Use the three basic questions:
  1. Do you want to sell?
  2. Do you want to buy?
  3. Do you know anyone who wants to buy or sell?

—Prepare your address list once, use it more than once.

—Always follow-up on the General Listing letter.

—Don't skimp on quality.

—Make sure every letter is perfect. Sign them yourself. They are a reflection of you.

—Work with your printer to avoid a form letter look.

—Don't put the property address on a Recently Listed letter.

7

How to Reap the Greatest Benefit
from Your Advertising

Advertising has two purposes:
1. To get listings, and
2. To find buyers.

Many salesmen fail to get maximum success from their advertising because they see it as having the sole purpose of turning up buyers. Finding buyers is important, but if it is the only role you assign to your advertising, you will get only about half of what you should from your advertising dollar. In this chapter you will find that it is possible to advertise for buyers and make a lasting impression in the mind of sellers.

THE CLASSIFIED AD

There are many advertising vehicles available to you. Radio, television, billboards, direct mail, brochures and newspaper classified are only a few of them. The newspaper classified ad outranks all other methods in importance and it is the subject of this chapter. Direct mail was discussed in Chapter 6 and the role of brochures is covered in Chapter 8.

Getting Listings

There is nothing more hopeless than advertising for listings. It doesn't work. Psychologically it is all wrong. If you run a general "listings wanted" ad in your local paper you are advertising the fact that your present selection of property is inadequate. Buyers will see the ad and stay away in droves. Sellers won't respond either. If you're running an ad for listings it can only mean that few people list with you; you're desperate. No seller wants to call a loser.

The Ordinary Ad

This is run in the section of the paper appropriate to the type of property being advertised. That is, a group of stores is run in the commercial property section, apartments are run in the apartment section. The ad looks just like any one of the thousands of others that are running on any given day. An example of the ordinary ad appears below:

> Fifteen year lease, nationally-known tenant. $14,000 net
> income. $145,000. Some trade considered. J. B. Smith Co.
> Call 880-2200.

Such ads have their place if all you want is a buyer. But they do nothing to create an image in the mind of sellers. There is nothing in such advertising to distinguish you from all the other brokers.

Many sellers read the classified before calling a broker to handle their property. A seller could read a hundred ads, like the one above, and never get the impression that you are the active, dominant broker in the area. The standard scatter ad in classified does little or nothing to build your image. It can, if you use your imagination.

Institutionalize Your Ads

All advertising must return a profit for the dollars spent on it. That is, you should not advertise just to get your name in front of the public. Such a policy is wasteful and unnecessary. You can get all the image-building advertising you'll ever need through effective use of your classified. And you don't need pictures or fancy attention-getting gimmicks to do it. All you need is a straightforward, common sense approach to classified.

If you're doing much advertising you are probably running at least three to four column inches on the weekends. Many brokers scatter this around in five or six small, ordinary ads. All this does is get you ad calls from buyers. To build some institutional identity, consolidate your ad. Put your company name at the top, in large letters, and repeat it at the bottom of the ad along with your address and telephone number. Here's how it looks:

J. B.
SMITH CO.

4 DELUXE STUDIOS

All have fireplaces, 2-3 bedrooms, 2-2 bedrooms. All the extras for fine living. Unique—not just unusual.

999-7800

PALMS AREA—20 UNITS

"No vacancy" units unfurnished. Much-wanted fast growing area. 3 BR.-2 BA. owner's Priced at 7.4x gross.

999-7800

SELECT LOCATION

10 newly decorated units. Near Broad and Main. Quiet residential street. Fully occupied. Long term tenants.

722-9461

$30,000 DEPRECIATION

52 unfurnished units. Pool. Sauna. Gym. 18% down. 30-year financing.   818-6901

TWENTY-FOUR UNITS

In Carson. Professionally managed. Seldom a vacancy. All one bedrooms. $170,000.   818-6901

TRADE YOUR HOME

For good income and nice living. 12 Units and pool. 3 bedroom for you. Beautiful building to be proud of. Best of all, a fantastic investment.   722-9461

$7,600 DOWN

SEVEN UNITS in Anaheim. They're really nice. On major street. All full & easy to keep full. 3 BR., 1¾ bath owner's unit.   999-7800

SELLING AT A LOSS

8 Units with all 2 bedrooms. Fine corner on large 90x145 lot. Seller leaving town. Initial investment, $12,000.

999-7800

J. B. SMITH CO.

2140 N. Center	999-7800
825 S. Main	818-6901
100 Broad	722-9461

This format does two things for you. First, it builds institutional identity by featuring your company name prominently. Second, it may get you better position in the paper, depending upon how your local paper makes up its classified page.

The layout of this ad makes it stand out from all its competition.

Buyers find it easier to locate your ad and also find it far easier to read due to the generous use of white space. If sellers read the ads looking for a broker, you will look as big, or bigger, than any broker in town. Even when competition adopts this format (and they will if they're not already using it) it is still effective. A classified page, made up with half a dozen such ads, has quite a pleasant appearance and is easy to read.

A Profit-Making Edge

This format gives you a profit-making edge on your competition. All newspapers have a set routine for making up a page. If your paper assembles their page from the top down, your ad (in this institutional format) will probably get top-of-the-column placement. This spot, top-of-column and above the center fold, is the best possible position; it has the highest readership. You can always get such placement by paying extra for it, but this institutional format will often get it for you free just because of the mechanics of newspaper make-up and the aesthetics of page design.

If the paper makes their page from the bottom up, your ad will probably appear below the center fold. This is not good. You can't get it above the center fold without paying for special placement. (At least in theory you can't.) If you're a heavy, consistent advertiser you can often, by working with your advertising salesman, get the paper to move you up to the top of the column. All you have to do is ask. You can't lose if the newspaper turns down your request for better position and you might be surprised how often the paper will try to help a good customer.

By institutionalizing your ad format you will gain the best of both worlds; you will get more calls from buyers and you will build an image among sellers. Try it. It costs virtually nothing.

Display Ads

Once in a while it pays to step out of the classified columns and run a distinctive display ad. Some sections of the newspaper are particularly suited to this step. The financial page, for example, is well-suited to a regular display-type ad. If your city is like most, the Tuesday edition of the paper is the best readership day for the financial page. A regular ad, like the one shown below will sell a lot of property for you and help build institutional identity for your company.

TEN STORES

$95,000. $10,000 down. No vacancy. All on leases. Near 10th and Center Street.

J. B. SMITH CO.

2140 N. Center   999-7800

Regularity is the key to success. This ad must appear on a regular basis and it must feature quality property if you expect it to attract listing calls.

Domination

Domination of the media is an effective principle to follow. The institutional nature of the ads, so far discussed, helps you to dominate the newspaper. You will look like the biggest real estate advertiser in the paper, even if you aren't, simply by the style of your ads.

Some brokers have found even larger ads a fantastic domination device. If your budget will stand ¼ page, ½ page, or full-page ads, you will eventually establish yourself as a leading income broker in your area.

HOW TO WRITE AN AD

The critical missing ingredient in most real estate transactions is confidence. Just as the sale begins with the listing, confidence begins with your first customer contact. This first contact, be it on a listing or a sale, is often generated by your advertising. Buyers and sellers must get a feeling of confidence in you as a competent broker when they read your advertising.

Confidence can't be built through exaggeration. Ads that promise more than any property could deliver do you a great deal of harm. Such ads are often false and misleading and they attract the false and misled client.

Take a look at this ad.

SIXTEEN UNITS. All one bedroom. Furnished. $10,000 down. Shows 42.8% total return on your investment. J. B. Smith Co.   999-7800

Could any broker prove that this, or any other sixteen unit, would show a 42.8% total return? Not likely. Yet this type of ad is run every day. All it does is attract unrealistic dreamers and repel those who know better. Buyers, hooked by this type of ad, often get incensed when they find the return is based on bare minimum operating expenses with no allowance taken for vacancy, maintenance or furniture replacement. Confidence is destroyed before you ever get a chance to work with the customer.

Don't Exaggerate

It is not necessary to overstate the merits of a property to get satisfactory ad-call response. The sixteen units, used above, would pull just as many calls if rewritten as follows:

> $10,000 down. Sixteen Units. All one's. Furnished. J. B.
> Smith Co.   999-7800

Even if the number of calls is reduced you have nothing to lose because those who do call will be serious buyers. At the very least they'll have $10,000 and be interested in sixteen units.

Abbreviations

One of the great curses of real estate advertising is the use of abbreviations. These shorthand words are barriers to communication. They leave the reader uncertain as to your meaning. Abbreviations may seem to make it possible for you to say more in a limited space but this extra message length is of no value if the reader doesn't know what you're talking about. When you use abbreviations you are talking to other brokers, not to buyers.

Abbreviations make the reader think more about the meaning of your words than the meaning of your message. Don't throw roadblocks in the path of meaning. Spell out every word, make it easy for your reader to understand you. Contrast these two ads. Which one would you answer?

> TEN UNITS. Loc. in Long Bch. $10M in. inv. $50M 1st.
> Moly. pymts. $350. 5, 1's. 5. 2's. Great spnd. inc. Call
> J. B. Smith Co.   999-7800
>
> TEN UNITS. in Long Beach $10,000 down $50,000 first
> loan. Monthly payments $350. Great spendable income.
> J. B. Smith Co.   999-7800

Eliminate Commas

Commas are useful in prose writing but are of limited use in ad writing. Ad copy must move. Short, choppy sentences communicate.

Long sentences divided by commas, make your message ramble and tend to get your reader lost in a forest of words. Use a period whenever you need a comma. Compare these ads:

Commas

MONEY MACHINE

Fifty units for $380,000 in Miracle City. At 6.14 gross with $45,000 down, it shows 10% spendable income, plus tax shelter.
J. B. Smith Co.   999-7800

Periods

MONEY MACHINE

FIFTY UNITS. $45,000 down. 6.14 times gross. 10% spendable. Tax shelter. In Miracle City.
J. B. Smith Co.   999-7800

Use Headlines

Headlines increase readership. Yet few brokers set their ads up with a headline. When you run ads (such as the example above) with headlines you attract attention. One caution, don't use subheads and sub-sub-heads. Use one strong headline and leave it at that. Avoid, for example:

MONEY MACHINE (headline)

45,000 down—$380,000 (sub-head)
Ten-year second (sub-sub-head)

Fifty units. In Miracle City. 6.1 times gross. 30 one-bedroom units. 20 two's.
J. B. Smith Co.   999-7800

Such an ad is too busy. It strains too much for attention and in the process it loses the reader.

Four Essential Advertising Elements

There are four things of interest to a reader:

1. Price
2. Location
3. Terms
4. How many.

If you leave one, or more, of these elements out you give the reader a reason to call. This ad tells all, there's no reason for the reader to call:

Five Stores. 625 Center Street. $45,000 full price. $8,000
down. Good return.
J. B. Smith Co.   999-7800

It has price ($45,000), location (625 Center), terms ($8,000 down)
and how many (five stores). It would pull calls if written as follows:

FIVE STORES. $8,000 down. $4300 net income. One of
our best areas. J. B. Smith Co.   999-7800

In this example I used:

1. Location (very generally)
2. Terms and,
3. How many

I did not mention price. The reader will call to get the balance of
the information. Think about this price, location, terms and how
many idea. It's a convenient structure for an ad; it will make your
ad writing job easier.

HANDLING AD CALLS

The main purpose of an ad is to get the phone to ring. Once the
customer calls, the ad has done its work, contact has been made. If
your phones are ringing but you're not making sales, don't blame the
advertising. It's doing the job expected of it. The weakness may
exist in the way you handle the ad call.

Proper handling of ad calls is part of your success pattern. To
handle an ad call correctly you must first keep in mind the one, and
only, purpose of an ad call. That is:

TO GET AN APPOINTMENT.

Ad calls have no other purpose. Unless this concept is branded
into your mind, your thinking about ad calls will always be fuzzy.
Here's how the top-earners handle an ad call.

The Procedure

The phone rings. You answer. Your objective: To get an appointment. Your procedure:

1. Identify your company. "J. B. Smith Co."
2. Let the caller speak. "I'm calling on that store you advertised for
   $3,000 down."

3. You reply by confirming buyer's wisdom. "Yes sir, that's an interesting investment."
4. Now buy some time and get the caller's name. "May I place you on hold while I get the file on that property? My name is John Brown, what is your name, please?"
5. Get the file and return to the line. "What information may I give you, Mr. Young?"
6. Let the caller ask a question. "How much is it?"
7. Answer the question and ask him one. "It is $21,000 Mr. Young. Is this about the size of investment you're looking for?"
8. Now he has to answer and you're in control. "Well, actually I want a place for my own business. What's the address?"
9. Now you've got another question to answer. Make it the last one. "It's near Second and Main, Mr. Young. We have several small stores available now. Could we get together tomorrow at 10:00 or 11:00 o'clock to look at them?"
10. He may give you an appointment right then and there. If not the buyer will counter with something like this: "I'm not sure, Mr. Brown, I think I'd like a little more detail first."
11. Now you've got him! "Fine Mr. Young, that's the main reason I'd like to see you tomorrow. I'll have complete details on two or three small stores which you can examine fully. Would 10:00 or 11:00 o'clock be best?"

You'll get your appointment. Don't forget to get his address.

Two-Question Limit

This ad call procedure has as its object the getting of an appointment. The meat of the method is to allow the caller to ask two questions which you answer fully. The second answer being followed by your first try for an appointment. The appointment request always presents an alternate of choice (10:00 or 11:00 o'clock?) to the caller. Most callers will choose one of the alternatives.

If you fail on your first try for an appointment, let the caller ask another question. Answer this question with: "That's another reason I feel we should meet, Mr. Young. I am free at 10:00 or 11:00 o'clock tomorrow and when we sit down together, I'll be able to go into detail as to this investment. Which time do you prefer?"

Hang in There or You'll Be Eliminated

Don't give up after only two attempts to get an appointment. Allow another question from the buyer and answer it by asking him:

"Could we meet at your office or mine to discuss this fully, Mr. Young?"

The point is this: After two questions put him off. Don't give out any more essential data. If you do he will eliminate the property and you'll never meet him. Most callers are only trying to qualify the property and narrow down the field. They're full of questions and if you answer them you'll knock yourself right out of the running. It's unlikely any caller will buy the property he calls on. What the caller needs is the dedicated help of someone who knows what he is doing. You're that man. Get an appointment so you can find out what the caller really wants.

What to Do If You Don't Get an Appointment

If everything fails at least get the caller's address and phone number. Say: "I'd like to send you some information. How can I reach you by mail, Mr. Young?" Follow this by a request for his phone number. With this information you can send him a thank you letter (for calling) and, later, drop in on him without an appointment.

Some Fine Points

There are some fine points in the use of this ad call method that ought to be considered. First, when you answer the phone, make it short. Give your company name and shut up. The caller is anxious to talk. That's why he called you. He isn't going to really hear much more than your company name when you answer. He only hears that because he's interested in knowing if he dialed the right number.

Be Brief

If you give your name when you answer the phone repeat it once or twice later in the conversation. The caller will be more likely to hear and remember your name if you do this because he is now more interested in who he is talking with. If your name is difficult or unusual, spell it out or offer to send the caller your card.

Don't answer the phone this way: "Good morning, J. B. Smith Company, John Brown speaking." It's a waste of time. Just give your company name.

Be Helpful

Be helpful and be cheerful. Cultivate your voice so that it sounds as if you are glad the customer called and you really do want to help him. Many men know all the right words but they can't deliver them in a helpful, cheerful way. Record some of your calls and analyze your voice. You may be shocked.

Thank the client for calling. Do this even if you fail to get an appointment. You might say: "Thank you for calling us," or "Thank you fall calling the J. B. Smith Company."

Hang Up Last

Hang up gently and hang up last. This really is a fine point but an important one. Too many salesmen forget to thank the caller. They terminate the conversation abruptly and slam the receiver down. Don't do this. Let your caller hang up first. After you hear him hang up put your receiver down. You'd be surprised how often a caller has a last-minute thought and starts to say something just as you hang up. You'll never know this if you aren't listening for the caller to hang up.

How to Get an Ad

If you do not write the ads in your office you are probably faced with the problem of getting your owner or manager to advertise your listings. You can ask him, beg him, or plead with him for an ad, and you may, or may not, get one. Here's a sure-fire tip which will save you a lot of time. If you use it you'll get ads without even talking to the ad writer. TO GET AN AD, WRITE AN AD.

Ad writing is a difficult job. The writer needs all the help he can get. If you try to help you'll generally get an ad. Review this chapter. Then, write an ad out on one of your scratch pads. Attach it to a copy of your listing and put it on your ad writer's desk. You'll get ads.

MERCHANDISING YOUR ADS

This part of the chapter is of particular interest to employing brokers. Even if you're not the broker, read it. It will help you make more money by working properly with your broker.

Use your advertising to help you list. One of the most difficult jobs an advertiser has to do is to convince his salesmen to use the advertising to help them sell. If you use the institutionalized format suggested in this chapter you won't have any trouble selling it to salesmen. They'll love it. And they will use it as a listing tool.

Use Proof Copies

Make it easy. Get proof copies of all your ads each week and give them to your salesmen. They'll show them to sellers. And you'll get listings.

One salesman I know had copies of recent ads printed and enclosed them in his listing letters (see Chapter 6). He got listings from it.

"This Ad Appeared" Cards

Ads play an important role in listing service. Send a copy of each ad you run to your seller, he'll appreciate it. Most sellers don't get enough attention from us once we have their listing. This is especially true of income property where the owner doesn't live on the property. He doesn't see us showing it and he seldom hears from us for any other reason. Send him your ads; he'll know you're doing something. A sample of a "This Ad Appeared" card is shown below. It fits a number 10 envelope.

J. B. Smith Co.
  Real Estate
North Center
Central City
637-7800

This ad on your property appeared

Date_____   Paper_____

Attach Ad Here

Every effort is being made to sell your property.

_____
                                                    Salesman

Sign It!

It is important that the listing salesman sign this card and keep a copy of the ad in his file. His signature indicates personal interest in the sales effort. The copy of the ad in the listing file is one more piece of sales service evidence, which may be used when reviewing your activity with the seller.

POINTS TO REMEMBER

—Ads ought to attract sellers; you can always get buyers with them.
—Advertising for listings doesn't work.
—Scatter ads (single ads) pull buyers.
—Institutional ads (grouped) pull both buyers and sellers.
—Feature your company name.

—Put your address in every ad.
—Get your ad above the center fold at the top of the column.
—Well-placed display ads can pay off.
—Regularity is the key to display ad success.
—Dominate your paper.
—Keep buyer and seller confidence in mind as you write ads.
—Don't exaggerate.
—Eliminate abbreviation.
—Use periods. Not commas.
—Don't use sub-heads.
—Use the four-element writing formula.
—The one, and only, purpose of an ad call is to get an appointment.
—Answer two questions, ask for an appointment.
—Always get the customer's address.
—Be brief.
—Be helpful.
—Hang up last.
—To get an ad, write an ad.
—Send copies of your ads to your sellers.

8

Profitable Sales Aids
and How to Use Them

Almost every time a sales manager or trainer mentions sales aids, there is a run for the nearest exit; salesmen leave the scene either physically or mentally, as quickly as they can. (The more experienced salesmen tend to run faster!)

Sales aids make most of us think of the old flip charts or slide projector presentations that were always prepared with a "canned" sales talk. Drive that picture out of your mind before you start this chapter. I'm not going to be talking about yesterday.

YOU AND VISUAL AIDS

Everyone uses some sales aid. That sounds like a sweeping statement, and it is. I've had some strong salesmen challenge it with a comment like this: "Not me, brother! I throw all the head-office visual aid junk out as fast as I get it!" Yet, there's no escaping it. You use a visual sales aid every day. It's the best aid you'll ever have. It's you. You are, and always will be, the best visual aid you'll ever have.

The Product as a Visual Aid

Many salesmen fail to see the visual sales aid value in the property they try to list or sell. Next to yourself, the property is your best visual sales aid. For example: If you're trying to sell residential or apartment house lots or acreage, try this—get the buyer out to the site (be it one lot or 100 acres). Tramp all over it with him; get your feet dirty. Then, use the property as a sales aid. Grab a stick and draw out the subdivision in the dirt in front of your buyer.

In the chapter on showing property (Chapter 10) it is suggested that you park across the street from improved property. That's using the property as a sales aid. Touching panelled walls as you call attention to their beauty is another example of putting the product to work for you. Using the product as a sales aid is dramatic; it puts showmanship on your side.

LISTING SALES AIDS

Listing sales aids may be divided into two groups:
1. Instutional aids,
2. Specific aids.

Institutional aids are things like printed brochures which help you tell your company story. They might also include reprints of ads you have run and they certainly include your company sign.

Also in the class of Institutional Aids are such things as: Greeting cards; Yardsticks (or other giveaways); Publicity; Speeches and articles about real estate.

Specific aids include, sales surveys, picture albums, testimonial letters, recently listed letter, the forms you use, your listing folder and thank you notes. The list could be endless.

The Company Brochure

You ought to have a simple (but attractive) publicity piece that tells your company story. Such an aid should be professionally prepared and printed on the best quality paper in the richest, most tasteful colors. Cut no corners in its preparation or production. A successful brochure, measuring 11x17 (folded to 11x8½), can cost 75 to 80 cents each in quantities of 10,000. If you're not able to buy 10,000 or more, your total cost could easily exceed $1.00 a copy.

How to Put a Good Brochure Together

Here are some success tips to help you put together a company-story brochure:

1. Make it as timeless as possible without making it sterile (for example: avoid dating your copy with references to a year).

2. Feature the people who make it all happen.
3. Show your facilities.
4. Show your training.
5. Show your supporting function—legal, accounting, data processing, etc.
6. Use lots of pictures.
7. Use a minimum of copy.

One such brochure, for example, is printed on a heavy, white book paper. On its cover is an artist's rendering of the company's head office, an impressive five story building. The front cover is bordered by a gold band about 1½″ wide. (It's the best looking gold I've ever seen. It ought to be; it takes three printing runs just to give the gold border a rich, deep look.)

The inside of this successful brochure shows pictures of the company president, the vice presidents, the attorney, the C.P.A. It also shows interior views of a couple of offices and a shot of a typical training session. Written copy is brief and to the point.

The brochure just described has been used for over five years. It has endured because

1. It's simple.
2. It's elegant.
3. It doesn't look like a visual aid.
4. Salesmen love it.
5. It can be left with the client.

Your Ads as Sales Aids

Pay the price for good reprints of your ads. Whether you run one or two half- or full-page ads a year, or a full page every day—get reprints on glossy paper.

It pays to show off big ads. Sellers love to see them. It costs very little to cash in on such a receptive market. If your company does not wish to pay for reprints, ask for permission to pay for them yourself. It will pay off.

Give-Aways—Delayed Action Selling

The list of clever give-aways, which some call "door-openers," is endless. (The Fuller Brush Company knows their value.) Some give-aways are like time bombs. That is, you place them in a potential client's hands hoping they will go off when he's ready to sell.

For example: A yardstick. I never met a family that didn't need another yardstick. They are kept and used for years. If your name is on them, you may get the call when it's time to sell.

A small blackboard that can be used as a message center has a timelessness about it that makes it quite good as an institutional sales promotion aid. Compare it to the relatively short life of such things as printed shopping lists or scratch pads.

The key to success in the use of give-aways is PERMANENCE and QUALITY.

Specific Listing Aids

Listing aids are like cooking; there's just nothing like what you get at home. Success-program salesmen make many of their own listing sales aids. One of the most effective and professional of these is the sales survey.

The Sales Survey

This is a list, by type, of the properties sold by you (or your company) in the last six to twelve months. It can be kept on columnar paper such as accountants use.

Typical headings are:

Address	Description	Listed	Sale	Down	Gross
————	————	*Price*	*Price %*	*Payment %*	*Income*
Times				Percentages	
			on	on	
Gross	*Expenses*	*Net Income*	*Down*	*Sales Price*	

The use of such information is limitless. It's immediately obvious how valuable it can be as a listing tool if you are interested in listing at the right price. It may also be used to get a good offer.

Picture Albums

Many brokers object to using pictures in the sale of property. I agree with them. Pictures tend to make us lazy. It's much easier to show a picture than to show property. Being human, most of us will take the easy way. The easy way does not sell property.

There is, however, a place for pictures. They can be used as a listing and lending tool. Here's how they can work: Make up an album for each type of property you handle. That is, one album for commercial, one for apartments, one for industrial, etc. Or, make one album with a section for each type of property.

These are albums of "sales made." They have nothing to do with current listings or expired listings.

Use two pages for each property. On the left-hand page, put an 8x10 picture of the property. Under the picture put the type of property and the sold date. For example:

Ten stores

Sold May, 1972

On the right-hand page put a copy of your information sheet (set up sheet) completely filled out with the figures at which the property sold.

These albums will become the greatest listing tools you'll ever possess. They will also be immensely helpful in dealing with lenders, who always want (but seldom get) good comparable sales data.

Letters

We all get letters from satisfied customers. When you get one, put it in a plastic holder and keep it in your listing tool kit. Eventually you'll have 5, 10, or 15 such complimentary letters. They are great confidence builders.

How do you get such letters? ASK FOR THEM. Write them for the customer if you have to. Most satisfied customers are delighted to give testimonial letters. The only trouble is they are too busy or too poor a writer to write one. Never fake a testimonial letter, but never hesitate to help someone write one for you.

Earlier (Chapter 6) I talked of recently listed and recently sold letters. These are business solicitation letters. Put a sample of each in your listing tool kit. Show them to potential sellers. It helps demonstrate how aggressively you work to sell property.

Your Listing Folder

Develop a sample listing file. Use it to show sellers how you service their listing. It's a dramatic way of demonstrating how hard you work to make a sale. Here are some success tips:

First—Use a printed file that has your week by week, step by step servicing procedure printed on the front.

Second—Staple a filled-out listing agreement to the right inside page of the listing folder.

Third—Staple a picture of your sign inside the folder.

Fourth—Include samples of all documents (completely filled out) necessary to make a sale. For example:

a) tax benefit analysis

b) ownership projection

  c) information sheet

  d) deposit receipt

  e) closing documents

Fifth—Include sample copies of ads run.

Sixth—Include any letters you usually send to a seller during the period of his listing. For example: "Property Shown" memos.

Include anything in this sample file that you'd normally find in your listing file. This simple, home-made sales aid will put many listings in your pocket.

Thank You Notes

Win or lose there's always a chance to send a short note of thanks to a client.

Develop a simple, fold-over thank you note and use it at every opportunity. They should always be hand-written and hand-addressed. Here are some typical short notes:

Dear Mr. and Mrs. Jones:

 Many, many thanks for choosing us to sell your property. We are already at work.

Regards,

               Bob Jenkins

OR

Dear Mr. and Mrs. Smith:

 Thank you for calling us. I look forward to working with you when you decide to sell your store.

Regards,

             Dick Anderson

The uses for such notes are limited only by your imagination, and the time you have to sit down and write them. Try them out, they'll put money in your pocket.

SELLING SALES AIDS

Just as in the listing aids, we can divide selling aids into two general types: a) institutional, and b) specific aids.

Institutional Aids

There are some sales aids that you may not give much thought to on a day-to-day basis but they exist as aids (or hindrances) to you every day. They are things like your building, your office, your desk and your car.

Your Building

Special attention ought to be given to your place of business. The day of the corner broker operating out of a shack is over. Our activity is growing up. People expect more from you. One of the things our clients expect is a facility that looks like it might still be in the same place ten years hence.

Avoid shopping center locations. Get in your own building in a top location. Give the appearance of permanence and success. Build an image. It will inspire confidence in your clients. It will also make your company a place where people want to work. Your building, then, becomes a silent recruiting tool.

Your Sign

If you had all the money that's been made off sign calls you'd be the richest person in this world. Yet, to look at most broker's signs you'd think they never got a call off them in their life.

Develop a standard, two-sided sign. Make it simple. Make it memorable. Make it right.

Don't skimp on quality. Have your signs done with automobile acrylic lacquer if you can; they'll stay clean and bright much longer and their useful life will be greater than the average sign. Costs will vary greatly but a 3x4 sign costing $25 to $50 is not unusual. Cost is important but if the cost of your signs ever becomes a matter where stringent economy is necessary you'd better stop and think if you're in this business to stay.

Make your sign simple. Too many brokers try to tell their life story on a sign. Do this:

FOR SALE

BARCLAY COMPANY

Realtors

637-0092

Do not do this:

FOR SALE

BARCLAY COMPANY

Realtors

Commercial Industrial

Apartments Leasing

Property Management

637-0092   1234 Example Street

Your sign is one of your vital sales life lines. It can also get you listings. If you get enough of them out you'll have a name as THE broker before you know it.

Here's a money making tip for you as a listing salesman: ALWAYS USE A NAME RIDER. Get a supply of masonite signs with—"Ask for (*your name*)" printed on them. Red letters on a white background are best. Black on white is also acceptable. If the broker is willing to put $25 to $50 into a sign you ought to be willing to put a few cents into a name rider to attach to the post just above or below the broker's sign. This idea will get you sales and listings.

Specific Selling Aids

Sales aids need not be elaborate. In fact, the best I've ever seen were those developed by the man who was using them. They might look a little homemade but they work because the man using them believes in them.

Don't wait for your company to develop selling tools for you. Success-program salesmen don't. Always be on the look-out for some simple, dramatic way to tell their sales story.

The Property Analysis

As the income property sales business struggles its way out of the dark ages of marketing into the sunshine of twentieth century methods, you're going to find more and more use made of simple computer projections. It makes no difference whether these projections are made within your own shop on your equipment or by an outside computer service. They are a fact of life today and will play an increasingly important role in the marketing of real estate.

With or without a computer you can use some sophisticated analysis right now. You can, for example, show any buyer the tax benefit of buying a property. This is called a *tax benefit analysis*. It might be for one year or for several years.

You can also work out an *ownership projection analysis*. This type of projection should show a buyer where he will be (as the owner) each year for the next 5 or 10 years. It is not practical to carry these projections beyond 10 years when we know (by the averages) that most buyers will sell in 7 to 10 years.

Such projections ought to show (in addition to the standard date): Equity build-up by year and totaled every five years, after-tax spendable and, sometimes, the efforts of inflation on the proposed purchase. Inflation affects income AND expense. The effect of taxes during the holding period and the costs at the resale also ought to be shown.

These projections are valuable sales aids. Even if you never get to present one that you make up they are still good because they force you to know what you are talking about.

Picture Album

The album of recent sales that you keep as a listing tool may also be used in selling. It is particularly useful in getting unrealistic or reluctant buyers to pay a decent price.

One caution: It can backfire on you. Some of the pictures may look better than what you are trying to sell.

Thank You Notes

When someone goes out with you to see property it is a good idea to drop him a short note thanking him for working with you. Here's a success-pattern tip: PUT YOUR BUSINESS CARD IN THE NOTE. Your customer may just give the card to another buyer or seller. Try the thank you note idea. Ordinary brokers don't use it. But, then, ordinary brokers don't make the kind of money you make, do they?

POINTS TO REMEMBER

—You are the best sales aid you'll ever have.
—The property is a good visual aid.
—Develop a brochure to tell your company story.
—Never skimp on the quality of a company brochure.
—Use lots of pictures in your sales aids.
—Use reprints of your big ads as listing sales aids.
—If you use give-aways, use ones that have lasting value.
—There is no sales aid so effective as the one you make yourself.
—The sales survey is both a listing and a selling aid.
—Picture albums can help you show sellers the competition they face.
—Picture albums may help you get a better loan.
—Encourage satisfied clients to write testimonial letters.
—Use your listing file as a visual aid.
—Use thank you notes.
—Your signs are sales and listing aids.
—Keep your signs simple.
—Use name riders.
—Tax benefit and ownership projections are here to stay.
—Always put your business card in with notes or letters you write.

9

Qualifying for Dollars

Qualifying your client is part of the selling process. The entire purpose of that process is to make a sale. Qualifying, therefore, is part of your closing techniques. Success-program salesmen are always trying to get a close. The better you are at qualifying, the more dollars you will make. The dollars you are qualifying for are your own.

GETTING THE PICTURE

It is essential that you keep improving the gentle art of qualifying. It is the step that helps you get a picture of who you're trying to do business with.

A Definition of Qualifying

Qualifying is an information-gathering process. It is the procedure that gives you the answers to these questions about your client:

What?
When?
Where?
How?

And, sometimes, *why?*

What will he buy (or sell)? When will he do it? Where? With you or some other firm? Exactly what location does he prefer? How will he pay for it? Why does he want to buy or sell? These questions are the essence of qualifying. The answers are all part of the big picture.

Qualifying may be thought of as a jig saw puzzle. You ask a question. You get an answer. That answer is a tiny piece in the big picture which is your client. When you get all (or most) of the pieces, you see the picture. The finished picture always looks like a commission check.

When to Qualify

Most buyers (those who call on ads) don't call to get something started. They call to eliminate your ad from the great mass of ads swimming in their minds. They are trying to narrow the field to those few properties that they'll have time to look at thoroughly.

The Telephone

Most salesmen do the same thing most buyers try to do. They qualify over the phone in order to eliminate the buyer! The first rule of qualifying is: *Don't over-qualify on the telephone.* Why not? Because it's economic suicide to do anything but the bare essentials by telephone.

Here's a story for you: We listed an eight unit for $82,000. It wasn't worth it. As manager, I wrote the seller asking him to call or drop in to discuss his problem. He called. And I really gave it to him. He got the truth! Among other things I told him (*told,* mind you, not suggested) that he had to lower his price to between $60,000 and $65,000. No one got angry. We had a pleasant, very straightforward talk. Nothing happened.

Next, I wrote him a letter. This time I suggested it was against his best interest (due to his carrying a second) to sell at too high a price; it also being against our best interest to "bury" a buyer, I enclosed:

1. A price reduction.
2. A cancellation form.

He, the letter said, could take his choice. Either sign the reduction or the cancellation. Nothing happened.

This customer and I had talked by telephone and exchanged notes; the action I wanted was clear to both of us. *Nothing happened!*

Nothing ever will happen in selling until a motivated salesman meets a buyer (or seller) face to face. Later, this seller and I met. He was a delightful man! After a few minutes of face-to-face conversation, he listed his eight unit with us at $62,500. It sold, of course.

Here's the kicker: Four months later he put a 43-unit in our hands. We'd never have seen that forty-three without that face-to-face meeting over his eight unit. Remember: It's dangerous to qualify by telephone. People do business with people, not with voices.

Meeting Customer in Person

You and your client must get to know each other as human beings. Until that happens, no real business is going to be done. You must satisfy yourself that this is the kind of customer you can believe in and work for. The customer, similarly, must see you to know that you are the best income property man he has ever run into.

To meet face-to-face you must have a place to meet. It's your place or his. Either way, you win. If the client comes to see you, he sees your magnificent, permanent, and business-like facilities. He learns something about you.

If you go to see him, you see his home or office and you learn a little more about your potential client. You'll never learn such things by telephone; not even if they hook them into widescreen television.

FOUR KEYS TO QUALIFYING

Above I listed the elements of qualifying, what you qualify for—what?, when?, where?, how?, and sometimes why?. The four keys to success-program qualifying are closely akin to those questions.

Qualifying Key Number One: People

You must qualify to uncover the person who can say "yes." Many salesmen fail to find out who the buyer or seller really is.

Here are obvious examples:

1. *Husband and wife*—Both must agree, but who IS the boss?

2. *Partners*—If they are all general partners, who really makes the decisions?

3. *Corporations*—If you're not talking to an officer you're wasting your time.

Let's look at a couple of actual examples: The first involves a radio station. The general manager of the station contacted us one day. His title: *vice president and general manager*. He said the station had to move its studios to larger quarters. What did we have available?

I took this customer pretty seriously. I chauffeured him all over town. He found what he wanted. A 10-year lease and a commission check of almost $10,000 was practically in hand. Just one little problem: This vice president *and* general manager couldn't say "yes."

The final decision had to be made by the president (in New York!) and I never did meet him.

It happens in listing situations too. Just last week one of my salesmen sold a property listed by another broker. The sale may never close—his listing was signed by a daughter. The mother, who is the sole owner and the only one who can say "yes," doesn't want to sell.

The second rule of qualifying is: QUALIFY FOR PEOPLE WHO CAN SAY "YES."

Qualifying Key Number Two: The Investment

The basic question here is: What does the client want? Most buyers don't really know what they want. I wish I had all the money that has been earned by clever qualifiers who took buyers who asked for triple net, triple A investments and sold them something else.

Buyers seem to think in terms of buying a building or a type of tenant, rather than in terms of their investment objectives. Good qualifiers get below the surface and deal with the real problem: What will whatever you buy do for you?

Sellers are a unique problem. Most of them seem to know what they want—too much! But, many sellers are as confused about their objectives as are the buyers. Here's a good qualifying question to use on sellers: "What do you want us to do for you?"

For example: I recently called on a fine old gentleman. He owns a shopping center. His tenants include a bank, a nationally-known restaurant, and several small triple A tenants in an office building. He also had a new group of nine stores, in the center, mostly vacant.

During our first call I sparred around for about ten minutes getting nowhere. Finally, I asked: "Mr. Robinson, what do you want us to do for you?" I thought his answer would be: "Lease, the vacant."

Surprisingly his answer was: "Mr. Allen, I want you to sell this center. I'm getting old. My son is gone. I have no one. I want *out* from under this, so I can enjoy the time I have left." He wanted to stay on, however, and do his own leasing until I got the center sold. This man knew what he wanted. Many sellers don't. If there is the slightest confusion in your mind about the possible assignment, then ask: "What do you want us to do for you?"

The third rule of qualifying is: QUALIFY FOR THE INVESTMENT.

Qualifying Key Number Three: When

Talk is cheap. When will they act? That's the key that many salesmen miss.

You are not in the conversation business. You are not in the entertainment business. You are not in the touring business. You *are* in the business of making sales. Here are some questions to ask:

"Mr. Jones, if I find what you want *today* (emphasis on today) will you buy it?"

"If we agree upon a fair price will you list it *today?*"

The essence of these questions is their directness. When you're qualifying for time (*when will they act?*) don't leave them a way out. Make the question clear; get a definite answer.

The fourth rule of qualifying is: ALWAYS QUALIFY FOR *WHEN*.

Qualifying Key Number Four: Money

With a buyer, it's this: Has he got the money?

With a seller, it's: How much does he want?

There's more to money than cash in the bank. A buyer needs some of that, of course. Your buyer also needs borrowing power; he must be a good credit risk. When you qualify for money, qualify for both cash (how much they have) and credit (how much they can get).

Sellers often want more cash than the sale of their property can generate. They may not, however, need the cash. There is an important difference between *want* and *need*. It is best to find out exactly what sellers expect a sale to do for them. If it can't be done, tell them so. Most of them know the truth before you tell them anyway.

Sellers ought to be qualified for credit also. How much secondary financing will they carry? Find out. Financing is often the backbone of your transaction.

The fifth rule of qualifying: ALWAYS QUALIFY FOR MONEY AND CREDIT.

SUCCESS TECHNIQUES

Qualifying is the most artistic aspect of your business. It is a gentle art; it is not a third degree. It can be done directly or almost incidentally. The less obvious your efforts to qualify, the more acceptable and successful it will be. Here's how it's done:

Be Prepared

Once again, preparation is the key to success. It need not be extensive. Most qualifying situations are more or less standard, and for those standard situations I have some standard questions later in the chapter.

Many sellers and buyers are unique. The sales problems they present are special. For these clients you must be specially prepared.

For example: Let's look at a seller. In a seller's market we often run into difficult situations. Recently, a seller for whom I had obtained a virtually as-listed offer, refused to cooperate by accepting the offer. Why? The answer became a qualifying job.

Before talking with this seller we (all salesmen involved) had a conference. I wrote down all the things I wanted to know about the problem in question form. Here are some of the questions I needed answers to:

1. Do you have an attorney? Who is he? May I talk with him?
2. Have you ever sold a piece of real estate before?
3. Who do you rely upon for advice? Is it the attorney?
4. What is it you *really* want us to do for you?
5. Why are we having trouble?
6. Are you going to accept this offer in the normal, accepted, fashion?

I called the seller. A friendly discussion developed. During the course of that discussion I slipped in the questions we had to ask. The questions weren't asked in the order shown above; they are seldom asked in the order you prepare for. As each question was asked, I ticked it off and wrote a short answer under it. As it turned out, I had only to ask three or four questions and the seller started pouring her heart out. I listened. In five minutes, the whole problem was solved.

When you prepare in writing, it is easy to follow up any conversation with a short letter recapping the major points of agreement. Success-program salesmen use this technique. Remember this: If the problem is tough and emotional, leave a written record. It will save you years of courtroom time.

Ask Questions and Listen

Qualifying is fast becoming a dying art; principally, I think, because it is a conversational art, and good conversation is dying in our era.

Who is the best conversationalist you know? Who do you like to talk with the most? Think carefully now. Isn't it the man who says the least?

Next to his own name, the most pleasant sound in the world is a man's own voice. Capitalize on this truth when qualifying: ASK QUESTIONS AND LISTEN.

Did you ever run into a client who just wouldn't talk? It's just plain impossible to sell such a man. How can you get him to talk? It's simple: *Ask questions and listen.* Most salesmen, in dealing with the strong silent type, have trouble *listening.* They ask the questions (because it *seems* like a good idea), but then they get nervous; they can't wait for an answer, so they answer their own questions and the strong, silent type remains strong and silent.

The sixth rule of qualifying: *When you ask a question,* GET AN ANSWER.

Every time you ask a question, you precipitate a crisis. The client *must* answer. The question is a roadblock on the highway to your sale. The only way this roadblock can be removed is by an answer. So, when you ask your question, stop talking and wait for an answer. If you don't get an answer, ask the question again. If you still don't get an answer, check to see if the client is asleep—or dead!

The Proper Atmosphere

There is no one perfect place to do the qualifying job. With a buyer, part of it may be done as you drive to the property. Some of it may be done in your initial interview in your office or in your client's home or office. The place is not the important thing—the *proper atmosphere* is important.

Both you and the client must be in the mood for the exchange of information which is so vital to qualifying. Here's a telephone tip that also works well in setting up a qualifying session: Ask, "Is it convenient for you to talk now?" You might also word it: "Is it convenient for you to discuss this now?"

The "is it convenient" idea is of great help if you sense the slightest reluctance on the part of the client to respond openly to your inquiries. He may not be reluctant to do business; it may just be the wrong time to do business.

You can't work effectively in the face of distractions. Common distractions are: television, children, telephone ringing, relatives, visitors. If such distractions crop up in a call, the thing to do is *get rid of them or get out!*

Here's how to control some of the atmosphere. Take the matter of frequent interruptions by telephone calls as an example. Do this: "Mr. Buyer (or seller) is it really convenient for you to talk now?" If he says "yes," then go on: "We are being interrupted by numerous telephone calls. Is there any way we can get ten minutes without any calls?" Or, "Let's get out of here for ten minutes so we can discuss this without interruption." All distractions may be handled by a variation on the same theme. The basic idea: GET RID OF IT OR GET AWAY FROM IT.

If you can't do one or the other, give up on the call. A professional can choose his own conditions of work.

Qualifying the Buyer

As agents for sellers, it is your obligation to screen buyers and expose the property to those qualified to buy. Good qualifying, then, is not only a matter of conserving your own time to maximize your income, it is also an obligation you owe to your seller.

Here are eight good questions to ask a potential buyer:

1. "How long have you been looking for an investment property?" An excellent variation on this is the question: "How many offers have you made recently?"
2. What type of investment do you have in mind? or "What are you trying to accomplish in your program?" The idea is to find out if he is a speculative buyer, an investment (income) buyer, a well-organized buyer.
3. "Do you own any income property?" "Have you ever owned any income property?" "Is it for sale?" "Is it for exchange?"
4. "Have you set aside a special sum for an income investment?" "How much of your savings do you plan to put into this investment?" "How much money have you got?" If you get no definite answers to these questions, try him on for size. Say: "Here's one, it takes $40,000 down. Is that about what you had in mind?" or "Could you handle $40,000 down?"
5. "What do you feel is a fair return on your investment?" No matter what the answer you're going to make progress. If he says "10%," you might ask "10% on the sales price or on your down payment?" There are dozens of follow-ups to the answer to question 5.
6. "What do you feel are the important factors in determining a profitable real estate investment?" Most buyers won't have an answer to this one. So have some prompting questions ready. For example: "Is it location?" "Is it the equity build-up?"

7. "Are you interested in an investment that provides:
   - a) spendable income,
   - b) equity and appreciation,
   - c) tax shelter?"
8. "If we find what you want, are you going into it alone? Do you have anyone with whom you would want to consult? Who is your attorney, accountant, trusted advisor?"

The Client Card

Develop a client card. Enter the answer to your qualifying questions on that card.

The object of qualifying is the seventh rule of qualifying: GET TO KNOW AND UNDERSTAND YOUR CLIENT.

Qualifying the Seller

Many who list are not sellers. It is your job to conserve your own time, and that of the buyer, by trying to represent only those who truly want to sell.

Here are some typical questions that will help you with sellers:

1. "How long have you owned this?" (Can they afford to sell?)
2. "Why do you want to sell?" Don't put too much stock in the answer.
3. "Have you ever had trouble with a tenant?" This may uncover some real emotional reasons for selling.
4. "Have you ever had trouble collecting the rent?"
5. "Are the taxes current?"
6. "Do you manage this investment?" This is especially good if there are several owners.
7. "Is this investment doing what you thought it would do for you?"
8. "What method of depreciation have you been using?" By the fifth or sixth year (under some accelerated methods) he's got to sell or pay tax.
9. "Has this property been listed recently?"
10. "What did you pay for it?" "How much did you put down?" You already know the answer to these questions if you've prepared properly for your listing call, but ask them anyway. The truth of the answers or the lack of answers will tell you plenty about your seller.

The questions are direct and to the point. They need not be delivered curtly or as a third degree. If done skillfully you can ask most people anything and get an answer.

HANDLING OBJECTIONS

If you use the techniques suggested in this chapter, you are going to be a stronger qualifier. Many clients object to strong qualifying. Here are some ideas for you in case you run into qualifying trouble.

Trying to Understand

When a client raises objections to so many questions, you might say: "I am sorry Mr. Client, I don't mean to disturb you. I am trying to understand your wants and needs so I can serve you better."

Serious Broker

Try this: "I am a serious broker looking for a serious buyer (or seller). You may be that person. If you are you're going to have a good man on your side."

What We're Looking For

"I am sorry Mr. Client, I don't mean to pry. But, if you and I were going on an elephant hunt the first thing we'd have to know is what an elephant looks like. I am just trying to find out what your needs look like."

The Motive

Most sincere customers are anxious to provide you with all the information you need to help them. When you run into one who doesn't seem to be levelling with you—question their motive.

Why is it they don't want to answer your legitimate questions? Why are they playing so coy? Is such action typical of a sincere, motivated seller or buyer? These questions flash through the minds of most salesmen when they encounter the reluctant client. The only trouble is, that's where the question stays—in the mind of the salesman.

Try this: When something seems wrong, confront the client with it. For example: "Why is it, Mr. Sloan, that we don't seem to be getting anywhere? I mean, I ask you a question and you either evade the answer or refuse to answer. That's not normal for two people who are trying to do business. What's the matter here?" Such a question will unmask the phony. It will also uncover those who lack confidence in you or those who just don't want to do business.

Not Curiosity

Qualifying should not deteriorate into a relentless barrage of questions directed against a defenseless client. When it does, the client feels he is under pressure and he will fight back by objecting (quite strongly) to the entire procedure.

Often the client will accuse you of having idle curiosity in his affairs. This error must be corrected. You might say: "I'm sorry you've gotten that impression, Mr. Sloan, because I am not just idly curious about your affairs. I have a sincere desire to help you with your real estate needs. Before I can be of any help I must get to know you and understand your wants and needs."

MORE SUCCESS TECHNIQUES

You must avoid developing a lock-step procedure for qualifying. Qualifying is an art and an artist seldom lets his art become obvious. Try to set your qualifying objectives firmly in your mind; develop the questions you must ask, then drop these questions into your conversation with your client at appropriate, but well-spaced, intervals.

Story Telling

Success-program salesmen are great story tellers. This device (which is a great closing tool) is an indispensable tool to a good qualifier.

For example: Let us suppose you are qualifying for money. You've gotten to the point where credit is involved. You must know the buyer's attitude on loan points. You might ask him, "How do you feel about paying two points for this loan?" If you do you're committing sales suicide. You might also just say, "You know, the cost of this loan will be about $400." If you do the buyer may object, so have a true story ready.

Here's one: "No one likes to pay for a loan, Mr. Jones. Let me tell you about what happened to me ten years ago. I bought a cabin at Lake Arrowhead for $15,000. The loan costs of $300 came as a complete surprise to me (I wasn't in real estate then) and I screamed. I didn't know it was customary for the buyer to pay such costs and no one could convince me it was. So I backed out of the transaction. Five years later I bought another cabin, less desirable than the first, and it cost me $17,500. I lost more than $2500 over a misunderstanding about $300 in loan costs PLUS five years of pleasure and equity build-up. Sometimes it is not wise to argue over pennies and lose dollars." He bought.

The eighth rule of qualifying is: TELL TRUE STORIES.

Assumptive Attitudes

Assume the client is serious. When you do this, qualifying can easily become closing. The story just above is an example. The salesman who assumes he has a serious seller or buyer when he starts his qualifying does two things:

1. He qualifies better.
2. He succeeds more often.

Recently I had a man in our conference room. He was trying to make an offer on a four unit. His offer was too low. It seemed to me that the salesman he was working with had not completely qualified this buyer. That is, he didn't know whether he had a buyer or not.

I told the buyer the Lake Arrowhead loan-cost story to illustrate the folly of losing a good value over a few hundred dollars. During the course of that story I said:

"Mr. Evans, you're going to be selling this place in five to seven years and moving into something bigger, aren't you?" When he said "yes" he'd already bought it mentally. My assumption that he had mentally bought paid off. He raised his offer $1250 and he owns that four unit today.

Another example of the assumptive attitude at work is this question which you can use on sellers: "When we sell this for you, what are you going to do?"

If you are ever put off by a seller or buyer it might be that you just don't have a seller or buyer; you just think you have. Try this: "We seem to be in agreement, Mr. Roberts. You say you'll be in tomorrow to go through with it. I assume then that *we have a business deal*. Is that right? Let's shake on it."

The words "we have a business deal" and the act of shaking on it seems to set up a powerful personal contract. It is both a qualifying and a closing tool.

Not Qualified

If your prospect does not qualify, get out. Don't show him property even if he seems to be a buyer. Don't list his property even if he claims to be a seller.

Be courteous, but get out! You haven't got time to spend with unqualified sellers or buyers. Don't burn any bridges behind you; always leave the road clear for a resumption of the relationship when they are ready to do business.

The ninth rule of qualifying is: IF THEY DON'T QUALIFY, GET OUT.

POINTS TO REMEMBER

—Qualifying is part of closing.
—Qualifying is an art.
—Ask: What? When? Where? How? Why?
—Good qualifying is like putting a jig saw puzzle together.
—Most ad callers call to eliminate the property.
—Don't over-qualify on the telephone.
—Nothing happens until you get face-to-face.
—Find the person who can say "yes."
—Most buyers don't have a clear idea of what they want.
—Most sellers know what they want: they want too much.
—Qualify for "when." We are not in the conversation business.
—When you qualify for "when," be direct.
—Qualify for cash and credit.
—Preparation is the key to success.
—For special qualifying jobs, write down what you must find out.
—Ask questions and listen.
—Don't answer your own questions.
—When you ask a question get an answer.
—There is no perfect place to qualify.
—Use: "Is it convenient to talk now?"
—Get rid of distractions.
—Good qualifying is an obligation you owe to your seller.
—Find out who the advisors are.
—Get to know and understand your client.
—Be a serious broker and your sellers and buyers will take you seriously.
—Sincere clients want you to know them.
—Qualifying is not a third degree.
—Use the story-telling technique to overcome objections.
—Assume that people want to do business.
—If delayed, shake hands on it and say "we have a business deal."
—If they don't qualify don't work with them.

10

Showing Property Successfully *

Showing property is not a part of the qualifying process. You don't use the property to qualify the buyer; you qualify the buyer and then you show him the right property. The first rule of showing is: *If they don't qualify, don't show.*

Success-program salesmen recognize the truth of this principle; it's part of their success pattern. The real "pro" seldom uses the property as a qualifying device, it's inefficient and unprofessional.

Prepare Before You Show

The second rule of showing is: *Never, never, never show a property cold.* Don't see a property for the first time with your buyer. Such a practice is an insult to the buyer, it destroys whatever confidence he may have developed in you.

In income property sales the top men are on top because they know what they are talking about. They never show a property until they are thoroughly acquainted with all of its physical and financial features. Until you are steeped in knowledge about your product, you're not in a position to present it to anyone. Borrow this idea from the best men in the business: KNOW BEFORE YOU SHOW.

The first step in your preparation to show a property is to see it yourself—by yourself! Too many salesmen depend upon office cara-

---

* Some of the material on showing property is republished by permission of the California Real Estate Association, from *Apartment Houses* (Chapter 2, John B. Allen) published 1968.

vans or previews to see the inventory. You never really see property this way. About all you accomplish in a group viewing is to learn the location of the property. Such an exposure also serves to spark your initial interest. But once you know where the property is, and your interest has been aroused you must see it alone. Only in this way will you ever know enough about it to sell it.

Groups seldom have time for a careful, thoughtful inspection of any property. Most salesman groups are more interested in the next coffee stop than they are in the property. When you are by yourself, you can spend as much time as you want learning about the investment. You are free of group pressure and able to concentrate on the only thing that matters at this point—learning your product.

Your Physical Inspection

What are you looking for when you inspect the property alone? You want to see and learn everything that could affect the sale of the property. You are interested in good and bad alike. Many sales fall apart because of the buyer's sudden discovery of some bad feature or condition of the property. Had you known about the situation, you could have overcome it by working it into your sales presentation. You might have even turned the undesirable feature or condition into an advantage and made it a strong selling point.

For example: You are selling an apartment building. Arrangements have been made to show one apartment until an offer is received, at which time the purchaser will be able to inspect all units. This apartment really sparkles. Your independent inspection, however, turns up that several of the other apartments are in need of painting. You also discover that these poorly maintained units are rented too low. (It's unlikely, incidentally, you'd uncover such information in a group. The group is in a hurry, they see only the dressed-up apartment.)

It's easy to cash in on this seemingly negative condition. All you do is turn it into an advantage. Plan to tell the buyer: "We're going to see one unit in this building and it is sharp. I've seen two or three of the others, however, and they really need some redecorating. You can do this work for about $65.00 per apartment and when it's done the rents can be raised $5.00 per month." You'll make the sale and you will never see it fall out on inspection.

Here's another example: We once had a seven-unit which we couldn't seem to get sold. It had an owner's apartment. The living room was quite small. Every buyer rejected the building once he got inside the owner's apartment. One of our salesmen got well acquainted with this property and he sold it. He told every prospect: "I'm going to show you an excellent building. It has an owner's unit for you. This unit is really in step with our times. Everything today is compact and efficient and so is this apartment. It has a compact living room which will leave you free to enjoy life rather than spending your time cleaning."

Many prospects, of course, would not even go to see this small (he said "compact") living room. Those who did, never complained about it. The building sold two weeks after this presentation was developed. Before that it had been on the shelf for five months. The idea for overcoming this objection came to the salesman as he stood in the compact living room during his inspection procedure.

How to See the Property

You don't need an appointment to visit the property by yourself. Some men do call for an appointment, but I've found it unwieldy to do this. Once in awhile you get in more difficulty trying to get the appointment than you should. Many owners have never heard of such an unusual request; they've been dealing with ordinary real estate people. If you just show up at the property, the owner senses you are a serious salesman. The important thing is to get yourself over to the property.

Once you're there, what do you do? First, introduce yourself to the owner or manager and explain the reason for your visit. If you arrive unannounced, he may wonder why you're there. It's not unusual to hear the owner say: "Didn't you see this the other day when your office group came through?"

Your answer is: "Yes I did, Mr. Owner, but it's difficult to really *see* (emphasis on "see") a property when you're with a group. I'm working with a buyer right now, a Mr. (give his name—it adds believability) and when I saw your property I thought it might suit him. Before I show it to him I want to get *thoroughly* (emphasis) familiar with the investment. May I look through the unit we saw yesterday?" Then go and see it. Really look at it, carefully and thoughtfully.

And now we get to the real essence of your technique when you see the property with the owner or manager: *Ask questions and listen.*

For example: "Is this unit representative of the building? I mean, have all the units been painted recently?" Now listen because the owner is about to help you understand his property. If his answer is "no," then ask him to let you see the worst unit in the building. Why? Because you've got to know what you're talking about. If there are units in the building which aren't up to standard, you must see them. If you don't, you're not selling an investment, you're selling a surprise package.

You might ask the owner to tell you the worst problem of the property. Does the roof leak? Are there termites? Is it hard to park? Are there some poor quality tenants? Find out. Because, unless you know about, and sell around, these problems, the sale will never consummate.

When you visit a property alone you will uncover about as much information as your experience and technique allows. You must approach the owner or manager properly; he is the key to what you must know. If you are sincere and business-like in trying to find out the information you need, the manager or owner will cooperate. If you are just following a routine you read in a book, they'll know that too and you won't get anywhere.

Remember, your entire purpose in making your solo visit is to become so thoroughly informed about the property that you can sell it and keep it sold. If you tell the owner or manager that this is your purpose, you'll set the stage for a helpful attitude on his part.

Unless it's your own listing, it is unethical and unprofessional to counsel with the owner over his price and terms. Never do that.

There is nothing wrong with a pre-showing visit accompanied by appropriate general questions such as: "What do you intend to do when we sell your property, Mr. Doe?" The answer to this question can be very significant. It often indicates the strength of the owner's motivation to sell.

The question is not always answered truthfully, of course. Many times the answer will be quite general, a mere formality or a socially acceptable reply. Such a reply would be: "Oh, I don't know. Haven't really thought about it. I guess the Missus and I will take a little vacation."

You seem to be nowhere with such an answer. And you are, unless you probe a little deeper. Follow up your first question with another and keep at it in a friendly interested way, until you get a bit closer to the truth.

Once in a while the answer to your question to uncover motivation will be quite frank, as in this case: "I'm sick of this place. The tenants drive me nuts. All I want to do is get rid of it and put my money in the bank." With an answer like this it's possible you know something no one else in the world knows—this man really wants to sell!

You don't have to sit the owner or manager down and put him through a third-degree to use this question and answer technique. Never be so obvious. Ask your questions as you tour the property. Make them a natural part of your visit. Most of them are.

For example: "Where does that door lead to, Mr. Smith?"

"Oh, that's the storage room." (Later, when your buyer asks the same question you won't have to fake it and end up telling him it's the door to the laundry room.)

"May we look inside?" (Storage rooms often contain items of personal property that go with the building. If you find it out now, you'll avoid a lot of confusion and haggling later.)

Your Neighborhood Inspection

Once your physical inspection is complete, your next step is to analyze the neighborhood. Look at it with fresh eyes. The longer you've been selling in the area, the harder it is to do this. Pretend you're the buyer; he hasn't been around here as long as you have.

In your neighborhood inspection, you should consider the best route to take in approaching the property with the buyer. It is far better to swing through a nice residential section, when showing an apartment building, than to approach it through the nearby industrial area. (Proximity to industrial property is not a disadvantage, incidentally. That's where many of the tenants work. But, for a good first impression approach the property from its best side.)

Apartment tenants like to live near conveniences. Find out where the nearest shopping, transportation, and playground facilities are. If they're within walking distance, you can play this up as one more easy-renting feature. Heavy residential back-up is essential to the success of neighborhood merchants. If you're showing small commercial stores, you should know the size and character of the immediate trading area.

Your neighborhood inspection should also include consideration of how this property stacks up with its competition. (About as good? Better? Worse? Whatever the answer, you can turn it to advantage.) You must know how your offering compares with other properties if you are to present it in a positive way. Your buyer will compare, as you drive him down the street, and some of his comments will catch you off guard unless you've given some thought to the neighborhood.

(No use getting off on the wrong foot and having the buyer refuse to even get out of the car!) It won't happen, if you prepare before you show.

YOUR FINANCIAL ANALYSIS

Once you've completed your physical and neighborhood inspection, return to your office. It's time to sit down and quietly consider the financial aspects of the investment. It's not only the figures, but what you do with the figures that really matters.

The Set-Up Sheet

You must know every detail about income, expense, loan payments and the like. You must know them as well as you know your own name. If you don't engrave these details on your memory, you'll never be more than a second-string player. The real pros speak with confidence and authority about any investment they present. And they do it without a *set-up* sheet in their hands.

Ever had a buyer ask you for your printed listing or set-up sheet? It will seldom happen if you keep it out of sight. To keep it out of sight you've got to commit the financial details to memory. It is your constant referring to these sheets that stimulates buyer interest in them. Buyers are fascinated by anything printed. If you wave your listing sheet around enough the buyer will eventually ask for it. And when you give it to him, you've given your brains away. The buyer now knows almost everything you know and he won't have much more need for your help in arriving at his decision. With the set-up sheet in his little hot hands, he'll probably run to his brother-in-law (a part-time real estate salesman) and make an offer through him. For a good showing, keep your set-up sheet out of sight until you're ready to give it to the buyer.

Get the financial details in your mind where they belong and leave your printed listing sheet in your office file where it belongs. If you'll do this, you'll be ahead of 90% of your competition; you'll know what you're talking about. This technique builds buyer confidence. It will not only help you get an offer it will make the buyer listen to you as to the price he should pay. After all, you've trained him to listen. Ordinary brokers just let him read.

The Emotions

Many income salesmen put too much emphasis on the numbers; they're not the whole story. They are, in fact, often a very small part of the story. The suggestion that you become totally familiar with the financial aspects of the investment is not meant to lead you to the conclusion that this is the vital part of your sale. It isn't. If you don't know the numbers, you probably won't make the sale. If you depend on them 100%, you'll never make the sale.

The decision to buy an investment property is always an emotional decision. All facts, including the financial facts, are merely used to support this emotional decision once the buyer's initial ardor begins to wane.

In your preparation to show, you must consider the emotional aspects of the investment. These can be woven into your presentation to the buyer. This must be done deliberately. It must be planned. If it isn't you won't be able to time it right or deliver it with the wallop it needs. To use emotion you must *really* know the investment and the buyer.

Here's an example: The buyer is an elderly man. He's had a successful life. He is now retiring as the president of a small college. He's thinking about his children's future. He wants to leave them something. In short, he's a proud man and a concerned father. When showing him a small property, our salesman said: "President Smith, twenty years from today, when your children stand on this ground, they are going to say, 'Dad was a smart man'." He bought it.

Even the numbers can be emotional. Project your buyer's position five years into the future. Show him how his investment grows. In one recent case a $7,600 investment grew to $27,000 in five years. What an appeal to a man's desire to be rich! Yet, a very basic use of loan amortization data plus the possible effects of inflation on the investment.

SUCCESS TECHNIQUES

A successful showing is planned. Many buyers try to rush you into showing them something. Don't do it. Most such buyers can be slowed down by saying: "Give me time to prepare for you."

Set up your showing in advance. Always make the manager, owner or cooperating tenant aware of exactly when you intend to bring the prospects by. If you don't do this, you'll find many of them out, or unwilling to let you go through the property. It's easy to imagine what happens to buyer confidence in you if you're not able to show him the property once you get him there.

Go in your car. Never go in the buyer's car. Don't let him follow in his car. Never meet him at the property. If he won't go in your car, forget it. You are facing a failure signal. Get the buyer under control or drop him. Buyers who won't go with you are not serious. They are using you as a bird dog. Let them deal with your competition, they need the practice. You're going to sell him something.

Use Your Deposit Receipt

Have your deposit receipt, or other agreement to purchase, lying open on the front seat. (Buyers are fascinated by something printed, remember?) Let them see the form they are going to approve when they buy something. It won't scare them to death later, if they see it now.

Select an attractive route and drive carefully. Don't drive like a maniac. You're trying to sell him something. It can't be done if you scare him out of his wits with your driving.

Don't talk about the properties as you drive. If you do, you'll oversell him for sure. Many of us get too enthusiastic about the investment. By the time we actually show one, it's an anti-climax and almost always a disappointment to the buyer. They never look as good as we make them sound.

Leave your set-up sheet behind; don't carry it or any other printed matter describing the property. It distracts the buyer. It also upsets the owner, manager and tenants.

When you get to the property, park opposite it. This allows the buyer to get a good over-all view of the building.

Show a limited number of properties in any one session. Most successful men limit the showing to three properties. It's hard to stay "up" for hours on end. All-day showings are hard on you and on the buyer. Traipsing the buyer from one property to another usually indicates poor qualifying. It also makes the buyer think you have no other prospects.

Know which property you intend to sell the buyer. If you've qualified properly, you know which property the buyer is likely to buy. Zero in on this one. Use the others, in your showing, to bring out the best points in the one you're going to sell him. This is a powerful success technique. If you don't know where you're going, you'll never get there.

Show to all buyers at one time. Many wives act as scouts for their husbands. Few sales are made by salesmen who take these scouts seriously. If the decision to buy is going to be made by someone else, there is no point in showing the property to the scout. This is true of all scouts, but it's especially true of a husband-wife situation.

Lead the clients through the property; don't follow them. Most people are reluctant to intrude into strange rooms. Take the lead and the buyers will follow you. If you don't lead them, you'll find the buyers hanging back at doorways just peeking into rooms. Or, worse still, they will be talking to the owner while you stand around watching your sale blow up.

Last of all, don't smoke while you're driving or while you're showing the property. A sale is always more important than a smoke. Many buyers don't smoke and they are made uncomfortable by someone who does. This is a controllable factor—control it.

CONTROL OF SHOWING PROBLEMS

The biggest showing problem of them all is the secret listing. It can't be shown. In this situation the owner doesn't want his manager or tenants to know the property is for sale. This is murder. As long as this condition prevails, the property can't be sold. And, unfortunately, it's a secret that can't be kept. Eventually the manager or tenants are going to find out the property is for sale.

This problem should be solved during your listing process. All you have to do to solve it is ask the owner, "Do you want them to hear that the property is for sale from you or from a stranger?"

Your suspicions ought to be aroused by the secret listing. Most such owners have something to hide. Many have made promises to their manager or tenants that they don't intend to keep; a sale will get them off the hook. Your pre-showing visit will usually uncover this condition. If you can't solve this problem and get the property openly available, leave it alone.

Some owners want to be present at every showing. This is bad; they inhibit free discussion between you and the buyer. And, the owner often reveals too much about his desire to sell. The talkative owner pays a high price; he'll never get a top offer.

You must build the seller's confidence in you and keep him away during a showing. It's a real failure signal when the owner insists on being present at every showing. Too often such an owner is only using you to dig up prospects he can sell after your overpriced listing expires. (You and I know this is short-sighted. But it's done. The courtrooms are full of such sellers.)

Mechanically it is very difficult to get a showing time convenient to both buyer and seller. If the seller wants to be there each time his property is shown, he is going to have fewer showings. No spontaneous buyer will ever see it. Solve this problem by assuring the seller you will send him a Property-Shown letter each time you show. Most sellers only want to be there because we never let them know what we are doing for them.

A manager can talk a sale to death. Talkative managers (or owners) are easy to control. Tell them in your pre-showing visit, "I'm going to bring Mr. Bates here tomorrow. If he gets you aside and quizzes you or if he asks you a direct question, please refer him to me. Just say, 'I'd prefer you discuss that with my broker.' May I count on you to do that?" Don't let them dig the grave of your sale with their mouths.

A property must be available for showing seven days a week. If it can't be shown on Saturdays or Sundays, you'd better get a two-year listing because it's going to be a long time selling. Level with the seller about this and you'll have no off-limit days.

Other brokers and unthinking co-workers can cause showing problems. Condition your owner. Tell him you'll try to follow all special instructions as to appointments, showing days or other matters. But, it's not a perfect world. Sometimes an over-zealous cooperating broker or co-worker will fail to observe the rules. Prepare your owner for this to avoid a loss of the listing or further restrictive regulations.

In an apartment building it is not usually necessary to show more than one unit. In special cases, where one unit would not fairly represent the building, arrange to show the best unit and the worst unit. Such a procedure gives the buyer a fair look and simplifies the later problem of inspection. It does not, moreover, unduly inconvenience the tenants. If everything is discussed and arranged with the owner and manager, even the most difficult property can be shown to advantage.

Some properties aren't ready to be sold. They are too dirty, or they need paint or some other minor repair work. Advise the owner to spruce it up. The buyer will double the cost of everything he sees that needs doing. Shabby buildings show poorly and their price suffers out of proportion to the cost of the needed work.

Your visit with the owner, plus the careful work you do before you show his property, has a specific and indisputable impact on the confidence he has in you. When you later present the buyer's offer, you are not a stranger. Your pre-showing visit and work makes getting an offer accepted much, much easier.

POINTS TO REMEMBER

—Showing property is not part of the qualifying process.
—If they don't qualify, don't show.
—Never show a property cold.
—See the property on your own.
—Turn disadvantages into advantages.
—You don't need an appointment to make a solo inspection.
—Get the manager or owner on your side.
—Ask to see the worst.
—Try to uncover motivation during your inspection.
—Inspect the neighborhood.
—Do a complete financial analysis.
—Show without your set-up sheet.
—Memorize financial details.
—Plan your emotional appeals.
—Set up your showing in advance.
—Go in your car.
—Condition with your deposit receipt.
—Approach the property from its best side.
—Don't talk about the property as you drive to it.
—Park opposite the property.
—Know which property you intend to sell.
—Show to all buyers at one time.
—Lead the client through the property.
—Don't work on "secret" listings.
—Keep the owner and manager out of the showing.
—Use property-shown letters.
—Condition the owner to other-broker action.
—Get the owners to touch up shabby property.

11

How to Get an Offer

Writing an offer is but the third step of the process that leads to a commission check. The entire procedure looks like this:

1. take a good listing.
2. show it.
3. write an offer.
4. present it.
5. handle the closing details.
6. follow it up (after-sale service).

If you have good listings, getting offers is not too difficult. Collecting your commission check, however, can be quite another story. In my first ninety days in our business I wrote thirteen offers. In that same period I made no sales. It is out of these experiences, and others, that the lessons of this chapter are drawn.

CONTACT PROCEDURES

Our first contact with a possible buyer is generally over the telephone. (He calls on an ad.) Unfortunately, this is often the last contact we ever have with the client. If you are not writing enough good offers, the quickest remedy you can apply is to focus your attention on how you handle both your advertising and your telephone technique. If your ads are wrong, the buyer won't call. If your telephone technique is bad, you won't get to meet the buyer. (Review Chapter 7.)

Know Your Inventory

To get offers, know your inventory. It is doubtful that any buyer will end up buying the property he calls you on. To show him what he will buy, you must know your own listings and that of your fellow brokers. In a big office this can be quite a chore. Most of us can't be thoroughly acquainted with 75 to 100 properties typically available through an active office. To generate offers, you must narrow the field; concentrate on four or five properties out of the great mass of available listings. An important offer-getting principle is: *Zero in on four or five properties at any one time.*

In other words, have your own personal inventory. These need not be your own personal listings. They will, however, probably be office listings. These four or five properties are "yours." Each one excites you. Each is one you know you can sell.

Zero In

When you cut four or five good listings out of the pack, you can afford to spend a lot of time getting to know them. You can easily prepare yourself to show them, as was described in Chapter 10. This is part of the success program of our business' top men. They zero-in on a limited number of properties. Do this—you'll find yourself getting offers regularly and you'll sell 50–60% of your target properties. You'll be organized, you'll have a goal and, with a goal, nothing can stop you.

An Example

Here's a story that almost had an unhappy ending. I was showing a twelve-unit apartment building to a mother and her daughter. The mother wanted to buy the daughter an apartment house as a wedding gift. They immediately fell in love with this twelve unit. It had an elegantly furnished penthouse which the daughter saw as her first married home.

On our first showing, the mother said "We'll take it." We were all in the vacant penthouse and mother and daughter just sat down at the dining room table waiting for me to write it up. I rushed downstairs to the car to get my offer forms. But, alas, I had none in my briefcase. (I had not kept a pad of offers open on the front seat as I advised in Chapter 10.) I was frantic. I dug into the briefcase. Way down at the bottom I found a blank offer to purchase; it was crushed almost beyond use. Fortunately, I was able to smooth it out, insert some carbon and dash back upstairs to my waiting buyers. The offer was written and a $10,750 commission resulted. My lack of organization could have resulted in an expensive lesson. Only good luck prevented the possible loss of this commission. This incident taught me that, to achieve maximum success, you must keep this rule in mind: *To do business, be ready to do business.*

Get Lots of Practice

If you aren't talking to three or four buyers or sellers each day, you're not in the real estate business. To get offers, you must get exposure. This is one of the problems we all face. It's true in selling, just as it is in listing. You must get enough practice if you want a consistent income. Every opportunity to expose yourself to a buyer in a face-to-face situation should be exploited. It is a source of constant wonder to me, as a manager of income property salesmen, how often men go out of their way to avoid floor-time. Men live off the contacts they make while on floor-time, yet many of them treat this opportunity casually. Some show up faithfully, but boot every ad call; they might as well stay off the floor. The success-program salesman welcomes floor-time; he takes it seriously and fights for all of it he can get.

Lecture Series

Once you've learned your craft and achieved some success, there are many ways you can increase your exposure to the buying public. One salesman put together a four-week lecture series on "How to Invest in Apartment Houses and Make a Profit." The series was given in the spring and twice in the fall of the year. It was always attended by 40–50 investors. No attempt was made to sell anything; the series was strictly informational. It was a genuine public service. This lack of a sales pitch impressed all of the audiences, and the man who conducted the series never lacked buyers. He's been in the Million Dollar Sales Club consistently.

Teach Others

Another salesman offered his talent to one of the local colleges, where he teaches commercial and industrial real estate. His course is good and is similarly free of a sales slant, yet he gets a lot of business from this activity.

You can increase your exposure to the local market by writing simple, straightforward articles on real estate for your local paper.

If you do this, be sure to get lots of reprints; they make great give-aways and mailers.

Get Publicity

Whenever you put together a notable transaction, be sure to send a publicity release on it to your local paper. Include an 8x10 glossy photo of yourself; about half of these releases get published and they bring in business.

To get offers you've got to get out in public. To depend solely on ad calls for buyer exposure is a mistake; it's too slow a process. Try the lecture series, teaching or speaking to neighboring boards. It will bring you business. Even if it doesn't, you will have the satisfaction of knowing that you are making a contribution to your profession.

RELATIONSHIP TO LISTING

It is difficult, perhaps impossible, to separate your selling job from your listing job. A good offer has its roots in a good listing. If the property is well-listed and well-shown to a qualified buyer, an acceptable offer is the logical result.

Successful salesmen are aware of the close relationship between listing and selling. Unfortunately, however, many salesmen don't shoot until they see the color of money. They don't list to make a sale; they list to get an offer. Then they use the offer as a listing tool. This is a risky and unprofessional practice and, as long as it continues, our activity will never rise to the status it deserves.

An Offer Is Not a Listing Tool

You should not ordinarily rely on offers to soften up your sellers. An offer is not part of the listing process; it is a sign of weakness and a failure signal of the first order to use offers to do what you should have done during your listing process. When listings are taken at any price or terms just to tie up the property, you are certain to have difficulty collecting a full commission. And, without doubt, few of your offers will be accepted. With a poor listing you never know, until it is too late, whether or not the property is really for sale.

Circumstances often alter cases. There are times when the taking of an overpriced (or otherwise imperfect) listing is justified. Such circumstances exist in the case of the truly motivated seller who just can't be convinced to offer his property at the right price; he has to test the market to assure himself that he is getting the highest possible price. In such a case, if you've thoroughly counselled the seller and stated forthrightly and clearly your opinion of fair market value, you should probably take the listing. Such sellers want a sale and, if properly conditioned, will sell. In general, however, to take listings at too high a price or at unrealistic terms without indicating your opinion of value, is a dangerous and unrewarding procedure. It makes most offers a waste of time.

RELATIONSHIP TO QUALIFYING

Every buyer has a purpose. To get good offers you must know what that purpose is. One of the objects of qualifying is to uncover what the buyer wants and needs. If you are a good qualifier, you will find out what the buyer expects the property to do for him. When you know this you can show him property that substantially fills his needs. More important still, your presentation can be expressed in terms that fit in with the buyer's objectives.

Talk to the Buyer's Interest

If the buyer wants to get rich, for example, you can stress both the cash return and the equity build-up. You might say: "Have you ever looked at it this way, Mr. Lane? This property sells for $100,000 but your down payment is only $10,000. That $10,000 is all you'll ever pay for it if you handle the investment properly. The tenants will pay the rest!"

Or, you might highlight the financial performance to be expected of the property. Analyze the equity build-up and after-tax spendable and you'll be able to come up with something like this: "Let's look at this five-year ownership projection, Mr. Lane. If all goes as projected here, your $10,000 will grow to $27,000 in the next five years. Here's how." Then review your figures with him. If the buyer's main concern is increasing his total wealth, then one of these ideas should find a way into your presentation. An offer will result because you qualified well and you used the information you gained to advantage.

The Fixer-Upper

Some buyers are looking for a job. This type of buyer is at loose ends, he needs something to do. If your qualifying indicated you have this kind of buyer, an offer is just around the corner if you show him your fixer-uppers. Such buyers are usually easy to uncover. Many of them will come right out and tell you they want a place that needs work. Others will tip their hand by constantly noticing the things that need doing as you show them property. The only caution you need to observe with the fixer-upper or critical buyer is that he may not want a deal, he may want a steal. If he wants to buy too cheap, you'll have to condition him to the facts of investment life.

Later in this chapter I will discuss another important reason for good qualifying when I cover its relationship to getting the buyer's best offer first. The point to consider now is this: *There is a direct relationship between your ability to qualify and your ability to get an offer.* The better you qualify, the quicker you'll get an offer. And, the better your qualifying, the better your offer.

RELATIONSHIP TO CLOSING

So many writers, speakers and sales trainers have focused attention on the problem of closing that the idea of the close has become distorted. It suffers (if this be possible) from over-attention. The spotlight has been trained on closing so long that many professional salesmen have become confused. Many of the writers or sales trainers, in an effort to make the process of closing clear, have torn the close out of the context of the total sales situation. In dealing with it separately they have fostered, undoubtedly without meaning to do so, the notion that the close is a separate, distinct step in the selling process. It isn't. Success-program salesmen know from hard-won experience that closing is a continuous, on-going process. It begins the moment you make your first customer contact and it continues beyond the time when you get your commission check.

An Eager Audience

In general we as salesmen are an audience eager for quick and easy closes. Because of the importance of closing, we ask for magic formulas which will solve all of our closing problems. There aren't any. In response to our demand, some clever closing gimmicks have been devised. These formula closes make great material for various writers, speakers and sales trainers. They have a magical quality in the telling, but produce very ordinary, if any, results in the doing.

These comments are not meant to totally disparage the usefulness of some of the formula closes. They are meant to put such closes into perspective. Formula closes (some of which are demonstrated later), like the sum-up technique, "I'll think it over," the lost sale, or others of this type are dangerous weapons. In the hands of an amateur they are as likely to kill an offer as they are to make it. Even in the hands of an expert, the formula closes will not, by themselves, get an offer. There is no magic in them.

Don't Use Gimmicks

Don't rely on closing gimmicks. Think about this: Everything you do in the course of a sale should contribute to getting the customer's final agreement. This includes your attitude toward your work, your customer, your proposition. It also includes such seemingly irrelevant things as your appearance, your office and your car. The ability to close is closely tied to your listing policies, your qualifying and the way you show the property. You should be totally concerned with closing and measure everything you do against its effect on the close. When you do this you will not have to rely on sure-fire, one-shot closing methods.

Understand Selling

To get offers, you must understand selling. The very essence of selling is the close. Some men have been sent in search of impossible results by a half-way understanding of the close. They pursue each sales opportunity in a lock-step, formula fashion: contact, qualify, present, handle objections, and close. They are constantly bewildered by the unfortunate truth that the magic moment to close never quite appears. Some respond to this situation by forcing the magic moment to appear; they try one sure-fire close after another in a desperate attempt to get an offer. It seldom works.

There Are No Tricks

Selling income property successfully is not a process of pressuring a buyer into agreeing with you. There are no tricks that work. It is a process of building confidence in you and your proposal so that the buyer will rely upon your advice and follow you to a successful sale. Confidence can't be created or sustained by a well-turned phrase or a few quick, catchy sentences that trap a man into agreeing with you. Confidence appears only after much hard work and is only given to those who care more about their clients than they do about themselves.

It's a Major Decision

Income property investing is a matter of major importance. As salesmen, we are always anxious for a prospect to take action today rather than tomorrow. Quite often prompt action is essential. Buyers, however, are inclined to caution; they often need time to make a major decision. It appears to be natural for buyers to take time in deciding to act. It is a wonder they don't take more time than they ordinarily do.

Formula closes do have a place in selling income property. If used appropriately by a sincere man, they can sometimes help a customer make a decision today rather than tomorrow. Their use is justified when it is apparent that the buyer has made up his mind and it is no longer a question of "yes" or "no," but simply a question of *when*.

Timing

To achieve maximum success you must learn how to use time to your advantage. There is a time to urge buyers to make a decision and there is a time to work with their natural desire to think it over. The artist knows the difference.

Too much sympathy for the delaying tactics of buyers ("I'd just like to think it over") will destroy you. Too little understanding of these tactics will also destroy you. An awareness of the problem of proper timing, plus your experience in dealing with the problem, will eventually lead you down the right path.

Don't Test the Seller

The object of writing an offer is to make a sale. To make a sale you must fight for the buyer's best offer. It is generally an error to test the seller with a low offer in the hope that you'll get a counter-offer.

If you have a poor listing you might be justified in taking an offer at fair market value in an effort to get the seller to see his true position. This, however, is usually a time-wasting, unproductive technique. It makes the offer a part of the listing job. The time you spend getting an offer might be more professionally spent (if you are the listing salesman) counselling the seller as to his price and terms.

Buyers who seek to test the seller with a low offer are often disappointed. You do the buyer a disservice when you go along with him. If you've qualified well and you know the buyer's motives are strong, you should always fight for his top offer. You might be only one or two thousand dollars away from it. You must close this gap. The more you know about the buyer's wants and needs, the easier it is to do this. A recent sale illustrates this point.

An Example

The property offered was a small industrial building priced at $45,000. The buyer was a leading furniture retailer in our city. He had virtually no warehouse space. His showroom was bulging. Our qualifying indicated he had more stock on the way. He was desperate for space. The 5,000 square foot building we found him was just what he needed.

This buyer wanted to pay cash for it. And, like many buyers, he felt that "money talks." He wanted to offer $38,000 for the property. We had reason to believe (because of talks with the seller during our listing process) that the seller would take $40,000 cash. We were, in a sense, only two thousand dollars apart.

We prepared two written offers, one for $38,000 and one for $40,000. The salesman and I went to see the buyer. This is how it went: "Mr. B., we have two offers with us. You may approve either one. Before you look them over, I'd like to ask you one question— do you *really* want this place?" (He wanted it.)

I continued: "Let me tell you a story (a great closing technique). Not long ago I was involved in a similar situation. The buyer wanted to buy and the seller wanted to sell, but no sale was made. The buyer made a fatal mistake—he made his first offer too low. The seller wanted $58,000 (always be specific) but the buyer offered $50,000 even though he was secretly willing to pay $55,000. The $50,000 offer made the seller so angry he refused it outright; he wouldn't even try to keep the negotiations open. The buyer lost the property. I have reason to believe you can buy this property for $40,000. I am willing to take a $38,000 offer, but in your best interests I recommend you offer $40,000."

The Lessons

The buyer went along with me and he bought it for $40,000. An offer of $38,000 would have killed the sale by ending the negotiations before they got nicely started. The lessons here are:

1. Fight for the best offer first.
2. Use the two-offer technique to eliminate small differences.

3. Tell true stories (about similar situations) to help the buyer see his true position.

4. Qualify fully to get an understanding of the buyer's wants and needs.

"Would You Take . . . ?"

Some salesmen fall into the unfortunate habit of testing the seller in yet another way. Here's how it goes: The salesman gets a possible buyer. The buyer wants to make an offer lower than the listed price or he wants some concession as to terms. Rather than fight for a decent offer, the salesman runs for the telephone. He tries the "would you take?" technique.

The conversation generally goes like this: "Mr. Ryun, this is Joe Brown calling. I've got a buyer for your property, but before I write it up I wanted to ask would you take $90,000 for it?" (It's listed at $115,000.)

The usual answer is an angry "NO," followed by a vigorous lecture on the lack of broker service. The seller's anger is justified. The "would you take?" technique is an insult to him and a sign of disinterest and laziness on the part of his broker. The method seldom works; it should not be used by success-program salesmen. Most buyers will give you their best offer first if you simply tell them, "Mr. Burns, our experience tells us that a low offer doesn't open negotiations—it closes them."

A Commercial Example

The idea of getting the buyer's best offer first is so important that I want to give you one more illustration of how it works. The example concerns a small group of stores that were listed for $69,000 and sold for $65,000. In this case the buyer wanted to offer $62,500. I refused to write it. After talking with the buyer for over two hours, he finally agreed to offer $65,000 and he bought the property.

During those two hours my main point was stated like this: "Mr. Smith, we first were offered this listing over one year ago at $90,000. We refused it then since we didn't feel we could sell it at that price. My advice to the seller at that time was that this property should sell for $65,000 to $69,000, depending upon the terms of sale. My recent advice (at the time of listing) was the same. I know we can get $65,000 for the property. Because of my strong feeling as to the real value of this property, I couldn't recommend that the seller accept $62,500.

Such an offer would not be in your best interest. If you approach the seller at $62,500 it is likely he will counter your offer at listed price. I feel, just as strongly, that if you *give me a chance to buy it for you* (good words) at $65,000, that you'll probably get it. Not only is the property worth $65,000, but such an offer is in line with what I've been telling the seller for over a year."

The buyer was puzzled. "You mean you won't present a $62,500 offer?"

"No, I didn't say that. Your offer will be presented. But at $62,500 I will have to recommend that it be rejected or countered at the listed price. Is this how you want your offer presented? Wouldn't it be better to make a $65,000 offer and have me fight to get it accepted?" The buyer went along with me and, as you know, he bought the stores for $65,000.

To use the technique of getting the buyer's best offer first you must have sensible listing policies and be able to show the buyer that a strong first offer is in his best interest.

WRITING AN OFFER

There is no right time or place to write an offer. It can be done anywhere, anytime. The fender of your car is as good a place as any if the buyer is ready to buy. Don't stand on formalities. There is no special need to have an offer typewritten. An offer written in a legible hand is every bit as good as one that is typed. Many offers are lost by the failure of salesmen to write when the buyer is ready. To get what you want, resolve to live by this rule: *When the buyer wants to write—WRITE IT!*

Closing in the Office

Most of the time, of course, buyers are not ready to write an offer on the spot. It is usually necessary to return to your office where you can sit down in a businesslike atmosphere and go over the investment with the buyer. To get the buyer back to your office you must be in control. (In Chapter 10 it was suggested that you always show property in your own car. If you go with the buyer in his car—or allow him to follow you—there is a loss of buyer control.) If you lose physical control of the buyer, you will get very few offers.

Many men fail to write offers because they don't know how to get started. The way to get a buyer down on paper is really simple— just *START WRITING.*

The Order Blank Close

The old reliable *order blank* close is still one of the most successful techniques for getting an offer. To use it, just take out your offer blank and start writing. To make the order blank close work, you must ask questions the answers to which you enter on your offer.

For example: "How do you and your wife wish to take title, Mr. Jones?" He says: "Joint tenancy." You write: "Mr. and Mrs. Jones as joint tenants." Each item on the offer to purchase lends itself to such questions.

Sometimes you can ask a rhetorical question, such as "Let's see, the address of that property is 1234 Main Street?" You then write the address on your offer. You might say: "This is June 7th, isn't it?" as you enter the date on your offer.

As long as you ask questions and the buyer answers them, he is buying. In less time than it takes to explain this process, you can have an offer written. Once you've gotten it written, just turn it around, hand the buyer your pen, and invite him to approve it in the proper place. Enough buyers will go along with you on this basis to make the order blank close one of your most productive closing tools.

Review the Offer

Some strong salesmen review the entire offer with the buyer before inviting him to okay it. This is how it goes: "Let me review what we have here, Mr. Smith. This offer says that you and Mrs. Smith will be acquiring the property in joint tenancy. The price is $106,500 for ten stores at 1234 Main Street. You are offering $25,000 down and will assume the existing first loan . . ." and so on through each detail of the offer. Such a review is recommended; it makes the transaction clear and prevents many of the problems which often arise after the seller accepts the offer.

All closing involves pressure and the order blank close is no exception. If you run into a buyer who feels too much pressure when you use this technique, there is a simple way of releasing all pressure and retaining the buyer's cooperation. A buyer under too much pressure may say "Don't rush me" or "Don't put any pressure on me." When you hear this, here is what to do: just say, "I'm sorry, I didn't mean to rush you." Then tear up the offer. This is a dramatic move and it removes all trace of pressure. Then move into another close.

The Contingent Offer

A reluctant buyer can sometimes be closed by asking him, "Mr. Smith, what have you got to lose by making an offer? You can't possibly win a race unless you enter it and you can never buy this property unless you make an offer. Your offer contains one (or several) escape clauses. You may cancel this entire transaction simply by disapproving the property at the time of inspection. Why don't we (not "you," but you and I) go ahead with this offer and see if we can get the seller to go along with us?"

Such an approach will often get the reluctant buyer. It is a hazardous closing technique in that you "buy" the buyer's agreement by showing him he has a way out. Surprisingly, however, this method works (that is, the sale closes) a high percentage of the time. It should only be used on truly motivated buyers who are reluctant to act for some unknown reason.

"I Want to Think It Over"

Many offers get stalled by the very simple but deadly statement "I'd like to think it over." In more than half the cases when you hear this statement it can be overcome. The procedure is simple. As a first step, it is essential that you agree with the buyer. Say: "Of course you should, Mr. Jones" or "That's a good idea, Mr. Jones."

Your second step is this: "None of us like to make a major move without giving it considerable thought. I'm sure you're serious in your desire to buy this property. Before you leave, I wonder if you'd tell me what it is that you'd like to think over. Is it (no pause) the way you'd like to take title?" Continue with your questions until you uncover his objection. As you can see, you have simply turned his "I'd like to think it over" into an opportunity to use a sum-up closing technique. Try this system the next time you hear "I'd like to think it over." It will work better than 50% of the time.

I Want Advice

Many buyers stall you off with "I'd like to check this over with my attorney (or CPA)." You handle this just like "I'd like to think it over" by agreeing with him. Once you've agreed, there are two steps you must take to turn this objection into a close. The first step is this: Ask him his attorney's name. Say, "By the way, who are you working with?" or "We work with most local attorneys, Mr. Roberts.

Who is your man?" This will often kill the whole objection because the buyer can't give you his attorney's name—he doesn't have one. Or he had no idea of going to see him.

If you get the attorney's name, your next step is to convince the buyer that you should go with him to see his attorney. By urging the buyer to take you with him to his attorney you do two things. First, you increase the buyer's confidence in you by showing no fear of the attorney. Second, you make it possible to make the sale by being available at the right time to answer critical questions.

Never try to talk a buyer out of getting legal advice. We deal in important and complex transactions in which the counsel of an attorney can be vital. Keep in mind that while the attorney protects the buyer he is also protecting you. Very few transactions involving the use of an attorney (I've never seen even *one*) ever give rise to a lawsuit due to misrepresentation or other misunderstandings. An agreeable and cooperative attitude on your part will solve most situations where the buyer wishes to consult his attorney.

Don't Force an Offer

Offers should not be forced. That is, a buyer should not be subjected to undue pressure or induced to buy because of some sales gimmick. It is useless to force a deal; there are too many outs available to the buyer. Forcing an offer is also a disservice to the seller who might accept in good faith never suspecting that the buyer was high-pressured into the transaction.

The use of reasonable sales techniques to help a buyer reach a decision are very much in order. Most people need help in arriving at an important decision and this is where you come in.

An Example

Last year we had an AA rated tenancy for sale. The property, a four-acre industrial parcel, was occupied on a 20-year lease by a nationally known battery manufacturer. It was available at $220,000 with $60,000 down. It showed $9,600 yearly triple net spendable—16%! It sold in four hours.

One of the possible buyers badly needed the help of an aggressive salesman. This buyer bad-mouthed the property, running it down in every way possible. He was, of course, trying to sell the salesman on taking a low offer. The buyer wanted to try $210,000 with $50,000 down. The salesman wouldn't take the low offer, but he wasn't good enough to get the buyer to make a proper offer. The property sold as this buyer sat at the salesman's desk doing a selling job on our salesman. The bad-mouthing buyer was incensed. He kept saying "Why didn't you insist I make the offer you wanted?" Apparently all this buyer really wanted was to be sold.

Time and time again this happens. Buyers play it coy, salesmen don't sell and, WHAM!—the property is bought by someone else. The cry goes up, "Why didn't you insist I buy it." Most buyers want (and need) to be sold.

Believe In What You Sell

To get offers, you must believe in the merit of the property you are trying to sell. You must get excited about it. Your belief and excitement will be transmitted to the buyer and he will act.

If speed is essential, as in the last example, belief and excitement are easy to come by. Once in awhile, however, some of the old hands in our business treat urgent matters with an "there-always-another-day" attitude. When this happens, the buyer is misled into believing there is lots of time. With the good offerings, there isn't any time.

If you're excited and you can't get a buyer to act on a hot one, drop him (he'll cost you money) and go get another buyer. When a hot listing hits the office, it's a race! Don't be running the high hurdles while everyone else is in the 50-yard dash.

Try the Techniques

No technique ever devised works all of the time. Give each of them a thorough trial. That is, try them more than once. Many of us, upon running across a success technique, try it once and, often, we fail. We immediately discard the technique as unworkable. Success-program salesmen don't do that. They try each technique until they make it work.

POINTS TO REMEMBER

—Good offers come from good listings.
—Develop a good ad call procedure.
—Know your inventory.
—Zero in on four or five good listings at a time.
—Never miss an opportunity to practice selling.
—Contacts can be increased through a lecture series, by teaching, and by publicity.
—An offer is not a listing tool.

—Know and understand your buyer.
—Talk in terms of the buyer's self interest.
—Closing is not a separate, distinct step in the selling process.
—Avoid closing gimmicks.
—Make time work for you.
—Don't test the seller.
—Low offers close more negotiations than they open.
—Fight for the best offer first.
—Tell lots of true stories.
—Don't use "Would you take?"
—There is no right time or place to write an offer.
—When the buyer is ready to write, *WRITE IT!*
—You can't close in the office unless you control your client.
—All closing involves pressure.
—Never try to talk a buyer out of seeing an attorney.
—Don't force an offer.

12

How to Close Sales

Turning an offer into a sale is quite a trick. Some men never learn how to do it consistently. Most salesmen feel lucky if 50% of their offers result in closed sales. Success-program salesmen do much better. One man, using the methods described in this chapter has closed 26 sales (out of a possible 26) in the last eighteen months.

PREPARATION

One hundred percent effectiveness is no accident. Nor is it impossible or unusual. All it takes is careful attention to a few simple rules. The first rule is: *Never present an offer until you are properly prepared to present it.*

The Appointment

Your first step in turning an offer into a sale is to *make an appointment to present your offer*. It is vital that this step be done properly.

The second step to a sale is: *Present all offers promptly.* (This is rule two.) This step does not conflict with step number one if you've been on the success program all along. If, by some chance, you are not properly prepared, you will have ample time to become so between your call to set-up the appointment and the appointment itself. The point is this: Don't delay your presentation. Don't be casual about it. An offer is a delicate thing. If it isn't presented promptly it will die. Keep this fundamental in mind—time is the death of most real estate transactions.

Step three is the most important of all: *Don't discuss the offer over the telephone*. Remember, the telephone is to make appointments, not deals. People understand very little of what they read and even less of what they hear. No seller is smart enough to give full consideration to an offer he has never seen.

Many sellers must be protected from their own emotions. It is not unusual for a seller to reject an offer over the telephone because of some minor irritation (perhaps even the tone of your voice) and later accept the same offer when presented in person. There are so many uncontrollable factors in human relations why add to them? It is far easier to control a situation in person than it is by telephone. Success-program salesmen always control the controllable.

SUCCESS TECHNIQUES

There are several ways of getting an appointment to present your offer. (Some of them are devious and tricky—they are the refuge of the weak and unprofessional. They will not be discussed.) Here are the methods used by those who *succeed:*

Method One

You call. This is the simplest, most direct and most effective way of getting an appointment. Experienced men always arrange their own appointments. By doing so they retain control of the entire selling process.

It is not difficult.All you do is call and say: "Mr. Oates, this is Bob Jones. I have someone interested in your property. Will you and Mrs. Oates be home tonight? May I come to see you at 7:00 or 8:00?"

More than 50% of the time the seller picks a time. In some cases you might get: "Do you have an offer?"

If this happens, just answer "yes."

Should the seller ask for details, put him off. You might say, "I'm sorry Mr. Oates, but I can't discuss the offer over the telephone."

Never compromise, even if you have an as-listed offer. Don't discuss it by phone. There is no way you can win by violating step three. There are many ways you can lose. There is also no way, on the telephone, that you can be certain you are talking to the seller.

Method Two

The listing salesman calls. This is a compromise often used by the less experienced. The lister calls the seller and says: "Mr. Oates, this is Joe Brown. One of our men, Bob Jones, just called in. He has an offer for you. Can he come out to present it tonight?"

Quite often the seller says yes. Selling salesmen would do well to think about these points before using this method:

—How well will the listing salesman set up your appointment?
—Are you sure all the sellers will be there?
—What happens if the seller says "no" instead of "yes"?
—Is having someone else do your work a step towards weakness or strength?

A variation on Method Two is to have the office secretary call and make the appointment for you. The same disadvantages exist when you use the secretary as you have in using the listing salesman. You might also consider the possible negative situation you are creating by using any third party to set up your appointment. Some sellers think:

—The offer must be terrible or he would have called me himself.
—The salesman is a real snob. He has a secretary call me instead of calling himself.
—The offer can't be too important to him or he'd have called himself.

Method Three

Go without an appointment. This, of course, is not a method at all. It is better, however, than most of the cute tricks often pulled to get an appointment. If you run into difficulty making appointments, then try going without one. You'll find this a surprisingly effective tactic. Use it, until you get strong enough to control your clients.

Getting Ready

The first rule of turning an offer into a sale is: *Never present an offer until you're properly prepared to present it.* Being properly prepared is really not much of a job if you've done a professional job up to the point of getting your offer. Your preparation, in fact, amounts to a simple review or last-minute check of data and material already used in the listing process or in getting the offer.

The Listing Salesman

Let us assume you are not the listing salesman, so we can separate the roles of listing and selling salesman. How can the listing salesman assist when you have an offer? What is his position? The answer to these and other questions depends upon the policies in your office. We will assume that listing salesmen in your office are adequately rewarded and, in the absence of a sale of their own, are anxious to help a selling salesman.

Actually, when an offer is generated, a listing salesman has two options: 1) He can drop all his own efforts to sell the property and help you; or 2) he can tell you "I am working to sell this myself, please don't tell me anything about your sale."

Before you reveal all details of an offer to the lister, ask him if he is going to be helping or competing. If he is going to compete, don't give him the ammunition to kill you; keep your offer to yourself.

Listing salesmen do not represent the seller any more than selling salesmen do. We often see a two-timing situation set up where the lister takes the seller's side and the selling salesman takes the buyer's side. It's a stupid tactic. The seller hired your company to represent him; the buyer didn't hire anyone. We work for sellers, not for buyers. We don't want any buyer to get a bad deal, but our primary responsibility is to our seller. You will do the buyer a big favor by being on the seller's side. Complete allegiance to the seller makes it easier to get offers accepted.

The Listing File

Review the listing file before presenting your offer. Here's what to look for:

1. Do you have a listing?
2. How long has the seller owned the property?
3. What did he pay for it?
4. What will the seller get out of the sale? ("You get" idea)
5. Why is the seller selling?
6. How long has it been listed?
7. How many other offers have there been? When? How much? Why failed? Who had them?
8. How many times has this property been shown?
9. How many times has it been advertised?
10. When was the last time the listing salesman talked with the seller?

Many times, listings expire while we are working on them. If you get an offer on an expired listing, you've got a problem. You're working for someone who terminated your employment. In such a case your first step to a sale must be: Get it re-listed. If you can't get the listing back, tear up the offer and forget it. There is no greater sign of trouble than a seller who won't list when he knows you've got an offer.

The seller's motivation for selling (Question 5) is often the key to your sale. If you know it, your presentation can be planned around this motivation. You will, however, seldom know the seller's true reasons for selling. Don't count on the listing salesman to know them either. Many sellers are better salesmen than the listing salesmen and they succeed in selling the lister on many false ideas, especially their reason for selling.

Verify the ownership before you present your offer. It is not unusual for a lister to have obtained only one owner's signature on his listing when, in fact, there are two or more owners. If all the owners have not signed, you've got trouble. You are about to learn how a ping pong ball feels in a real fast game. This is essentially a no-listing problem, you solve it the same way.

A review of the sales activity is most helpful. Sellers are often more receptive to an offer if they feel an honest effort has been made to sell the property. You should know how many ads have been run, how many times the property has been shown, as well as every detail of every offer. The more you know, the easier it is to get an acceptance.

Prepare for Objections

Your review of the listing file and your talk with the listing salesman will turn up some problem areas. Typical problems are:
—special cash requirements
—occupancy
—secondary financing.
Whatever the problem is, you must prepare to handle it.

Cash is often the problem. It can tell you a lot about the seller's motivation. Consider, for example, a seller who has listed a $40,000 property at 10% down. There is a $3000 second to pay off. The commission is $2400 and there are other normal fees. The expense of this sale could easily run into $4000 plus the $3000 loan pay-off. There may be a problem here. Before you present your offer it would be wise to ask the listing salesman if he and the seller know it is going to cost the seller money to sell. It may be a surprise to the lister to find this out. You may be sure that it isn't a surprise to the seller. He knows it and he intends to cure it all by giving you paper for your commission. To avoid this problem you must recognize it and prepare to handle it in advance.

If the seller is willing to take money out of his pocket to make a sale (in effect he buys a second on his own property) you've got motivation. If you can't close that kind, give up.

The problems differ with each situation. Whatever they happen to be, prepare two or three ways of overcoming them. You may not need to use any of your methods (it's surprising how often that happens), but if the objection comes up it's your commission against your preparation.

YOUR PRESENTATION

There is no need to be nervous when you present an offer. Excited, yes. Nervous, no. You hold all the aces. You've got what the seller wants—an offer, a chance to sell his property. As you present your offer keep these rules in mind:

1. Be relaxed.
2. Don't rush.
3. Be on the seller's side.
4. Shut-up once in a while, and listen.
5. Don't "sell" the offer.
6. Don't mislead.

There are many other little rules affecting offers but if you'll live by these you'll do all right.

Setting the Stage

Never present an offer unless the physical and human conditions are right. Set the stage for success. Control the situation (If you don't, you'll be controlled!) and get everything set to your liking.

For example: You are presenting your offer to a man and his wife in their home. Where are you going to sit. Living Room? Kitchen? T.V. Room? Dining Room?

The husband and wife, of course, will lead you to the living room (generally) where they will promptly sit opposite each other with you in the middle. Don't let this happen! When you get between a husband and a wife (or two partners) you're in a failure sandwich. Get out of it before they have you for dinner!

You set the stage. Take command, and take it quickly. Even if you're seated in the "failure position" described, it's not too late.

All you do is: Get up. Walk towards the dining room or kitchen, and say "Can we sit around this table while we talk?" (In a business situation just ask: "Can we use your conference room?)

Be sure you sit the sellers down side-by-side, with you opposite them. Never let them sit opposite each other where they can exchange secret, meaningful glances which you can't read. When you've got them side-by-side, two things work in your favor:

1. You can watch them both, and
2. They can both watch you.

The seating of the sellers and the atmosphere in which you present your offer is a controllable factor. Control it!

All noise and other distractions must be eliminated for a successful presentation. Here are two examples: I once had a seller trying to watch a football game on television while listening to an offer on his property. Such a situation is impossible. Most of us can't concentrate on one thing at a time let alone two things. Here's how to handle it: "Mr. Jones, perhaps I'd better come back later when you're free to talk business." If he replies, "No, go ahead, I can hear you." Just say, "I'm sorry, Mr. Jones, but I'm not good enough to compete with your television." Then stand up. If necessary leave. Very few sellers will ever let you leave.

The same tactics are useful if you are competing against a businessman's telephone or dictation. Don't do it. Engrave this on your mind: *If you can't get their complete attention, don't present the offer.*

MORE SUCCESS TECHNIQUES

There are many cute and tricky little methods that have been advanced over the years by those who seem more interested in creating a stir than in creating a sale. Few cute tricks work. Good business techniques do work.

Your first step to success is to assume you've got a sale. Many writers call this the *assumptive attitude* method of presenting an offer. It's a good one. If you don't believe in your own offer (Why did you write it?), how are you going to get a seller to agree with you?

Work from the Bottom Up

The cleverest use of the assumptive attitude is a presentation method called *working from the bottom up.* It goes like this:

First—Wave the deposit check in the air. "Mr Smith, we have a deposit for $5,000 on your property. Here it is." Then hold it up so he can see it.

Second—Start explaining the offer. Begin with the most minor point. For example: "Mr. Brown has asked that the building be inspected for insect infestation (such as termites). That's okay, isn't it?"

Third—Move up the offer. Deal with the next small point. It might be: "The buyer wants a standard policy of title insurance." That's all right, of course, since this is standard practice (or what you agreed to in your listing).

Other steps in the presentation will take you to a statement like: "The buyer has asked that this sale close in 30 days. Is that okay?"

Up to this point you've got the sellers with you. It's a beautiful world of agreement. You think it's sold and so do they. You are about to move into the money area. Remember now, the seller knows the deposit amount ($5000), but he doesn't yet know the down payment. He won't for a while. Let's continue with our presentation.

Deal now with any minor contingencies and get the seller's agreement to them. These are usually things like inspection, rental statement, personal property inventory and the like.

Your next move is to the money. If a second mortgage is involved you say: "The buyer has agreed to execute a note secured by a second deed of trust (or mortgage) for $10,000. It pays a $100 a month including 8% interest and will be paid in full in 5 years. That gives you so-many dollars in interest (name the exact figure). Then continue: "The buyer will assume (or will get a new loan) the existing loan at his expense."

Seller Anxiety

By this time your sellers will be a little anxious or nervous. They have all the facts but, unless they are quick to figure, they don't know what the buyer is paying. You will get questions like this: "Okay, how much is this guy offering?" or "How much are we getting?"

Both these questions lead you into your "You Get" presentation. (See Chapter 5.) This method works if you believe this basic truth: People are more interested in what they actually get (now, in cash and loans) than they are in the price.

You might think this bottom-up assumptive method appropriate only for the unsophisticated momma and poppa situations. Don't you believe it! I've seen it take apart the most sophisticated sellers you'll ever meet.

Getting It Signed

The moment of truth eventually comes, just as it does in a listing situation. To get a sale you've got to get your offer signed. Here are some ideas used by the success-program salesmen.

Agreement Signals

In a husband and wife situation, one of the most certain signs of agreement is their request to leave the room. They'll say something like this: "We'd like to go into the kitchen and talk this over" or "Would you excuse us for a minute?"

If this happens, you're in. It's a sale. If it wasn't they'd tell you they didn't like the offer; they wouldn't have to leave the room to do that.

The out-of-the-room conference should never be prevented. It is generally needed to settle an emotional point (Who's boss here?) or some private money point. Some brokers encourage this private husband and wife conference by saying: "Would you folks like me to leave (go around the block, step into another room) for a few minutes?"

If you're a close student of human behavior, you may have noticed how people act as you present some proposals to them. Quite often your client will lean forward, with hands clenched, intent upon what you are saying. His whole attitude appears to be one of attention—it is actually one of *tension.*

How does he act when he finally agrees? First, he unclenches his hands. Often he leans back in his chair. In general, he relaxes. He is talking to you with his body. All this happens before he ever utters that beautiful word "yes."

Success-program salesmen are close students of human behavior. Borrow a leaf from their book. Take three or four college-level courses in psychology. It will help you as a salesman. Remember: When you see these physical signs of agreement, ask for the signature.

Getting the Signature

Most successful salesmen keep the actual offer in their pocket until it is needed for the seller's signature. This may seem to violate a conditioning rule (Let them see and get used to the document they are going to sign.) but it is a necessary success tactic. The reason? If you take out the offer and read from it, the seller may grab it out of your hands and your whole presentation plan will blow up.

It is often wise to fill in the amount of your commission before you leave to present your offer. There are two good reasons for this:

1. It reinforces your assumption of a sale, and
2. It prevents you from forgetting to fill it in in the excitement of getting the offer signed.

Once you've explained the entire transaction do this:

1. Ask "Have I made everything clear, Mr. Seller? Do you have any questions?
2. Hand the offer to the seller and say: "Please approve it here where it says 'approval of seller'."

Then, shut up. He's either going to sign it or he isn't. If he doesn't sign, find out why and get a counter-offer.

Counter-Offers

Here's another success-program principle: ALWAYS GET A COUNTER OFFER.

Even if you know, with the same certainty that you know the sun will rise tomorrow, that the buyer will not go for the counter-proposal, you must always write it up. Why? Because:

1. You can't be that sure of anything, and
2. You've got to get that seller committed to his best (or secret) price in writing.

After all, your buyer is not the only buyer in the world. If he doesn't like the seller's counter-offer, go sell it to someone else.

When you take written counters, you *know* the secret price. If your buyer doesn't buy, get the listing reduced to the counter-offer price.

Don't be selfish. Take the counter-offer even if it is not your listing. Tomorrow someone will break one of yours down for you.

CLOSING DETAILS

Quite often sellers get irritated by the many small details connected with the closing of a sale. Sometimes they refuse to cooperate in providing needed information or are simply too slow in acting and thus *they* jeopardize their own transaction.

Condition the Seller

When you get your offer accepted, condition your seller to the need for his complete cooperation in getting the transaction closed. You might say: "Mr. Smith, you might say you and I are partners in this transaction. As your partner I am going to do everything I can to make sure every detail of closing is promptly and accurately handled. You, as a partner, have some obligations too. You must provide all needed information quickly and completely. Can I count on this transaction being a good partnership?" Then explain some of the closing details.

The Rent Statement

Review the need for an accurate rental statement that shows tenant name, space occupied, rent paid, date paid to, type of tenancy, anything included in rent (water, gas, electric), security deposits. Success-program salesmen take this rental statement as the next step after getting the offer signed.

Inspection

Carefully explain your inspection procedure. It is disastrous to turn up with the buyer to inspect a property and be unable to do so because the owner is not there or has failed to authorize his manager to allow the inspection.

Many sales are lost because of careless inspection procedures. Here's a money-making tip: INSPECT IT TWICE.

First—you and the owner.

Second—you and the buyer.

This one idea could make you the top man in your company.

Signatures

Most properties transfer by deed. Get the deed signed quickly. Explain to your seller the absolute need for acting quickly on any document that requires his signature. If you need a notary, take one with you. Don't leave documents with buyers or sellers to sign and get acknowledged at their convenience.

Profit from this device of the success-program broker: *Don't mail a thing.* Take all documents to all buyers and sellers yourself and sit there until they sign them. The U. S. Post Office does not have a real estate license; don't expect them to make your transaction for you.

Follow-up

Work every sale over to get listings. Contact all surrounding owners and tell them of your sale (see Chapter 6). Take the new owner to his property after the sale closes and make sure he understands and is comfortable in his new ownership situation. Ask him for buyer and seller prospects.

POINTS TO REMEMBER

—One hundred percent effectiveness is no accident.
—Never present until you're prepared.
—Present all offers promptly.
—Time is the death of most transactions.
—Don't discuss your offer over the telephone.
—Protect sellers from their own emotions—see them in person.
—Call for your own appointment.
—If you can't call for an appointment, go without one.
—Make sure you understand the role of the listing salesman; as a helper, as a competitor.
—Listing salesmen don't represent the seller any more than you do.
—Be on the seller's side.
—Review the listing file.
—If you don't have a listing, get one.
—Don't put too much faith in what sellers SAY is their reason for selling.
—Verify ownership before you present.
—Present your offer to all owners at once or don't present it.
—Know the history of all offers on the property.
—Anticipate objections.
—Sellers who net nothing often try commission cutting.
—Present your offer like a businessman. Avoid cute tricks and gimmicks.
—Don't present unless the physical conditions are right.
—Don't let the sellers sit opposite each other.
—Assume you've got a sale.
—Present from the bottom-up.
—Use the "you get" technique.
—Watch for physical signs of agreement.
—Keep the offer in your pocket as you present it.
—Fill in the commission before you make your call.
—If you don't get it accepted: Always get a counter offer.
—Condition your seller to the details of closing.
—Don't mail documents.
—Follow up every sale for listings and buyers.

13

Cash Commissions
and How to Obtain Them

A cash commission begins with your listing. If your listing practices are weak, your chances of collecting a full cash commission are poor. One of the great advantages of working on exclusives only is that you generally get your commission and it is usually in cash. When you work on mere handshakes or verbal listings, you will always be in a dogfight for your commission.

YOUR PHILOSOPHY

Cash or paper? Half a loaf or all of it? It's all up to you. You call the tune and the clients dance to it if your attitude is right and if you are strong. Without a proper attitude and personal strength, cash commissions are impossible. Success-program salesmen know the worth of their services. They have a deep belief in the integrity of their fee. To a success-minded broker a cut commission or a non-cash commission is unthinkable. To them, any fee short of a full cash commission is a disservice to the real estate profession. They seldom sell themselves or their profession short.

To get a cash commission, you must adopt an assumptive attitude toward your brokerage fee. You must believe that all commissions will be paid when due and in cash. The idea of a cut commission must be driven from your mind. Compromised commissions don't exist for the man who refuses to give them life by believing in them. Your assumption must be that when you've done enough for both buyer and seller, your fee is the natural result of competent service.

If you assume you will be paid *you will be*. The very fact that you've made such an assumption transmits to all parties to the transaction. Your listing sets it up and your attitude and conduct throughout the negotiations maintain your cash commission position. It is seldom necessary to make a major point of your commission if you conduct all of your buyer and seller contacts in a businesslike way.

Many salesmen fail to get full cash commissions because they don't expect them. They are defeated before they start. The world has worn them down. They've throw up their hands and surrendered to the very natural desire of buyers and sellers to get off as cheaply as possible. If you become convinced no one pays in cash and all commissions are cut, you're right—they all will be.

Half a Loaf, or None?

There is an old maxim—half a loaf is better than none—that has done our business more harm than, perhaps, any other false idea. Half a loaf is *not* better than none; it is *worse* than none. You can't run your business on half commissions. You can't keep your own self-respect and be a commission-cutter. Taking a half loaf is the desperate measure of a desperate man. It is a sign of weakness. It is a failure signal that can't be disregarded. Every time you cut a commission or take something other than cash as your fee, you have lost. There is no such thing as half a victory. You either win or you lose. When you cut, you lose!

Negative Education

Most commission-cutters have a puzzling attitude toward their fee. They truly feel that something is better than nothing. It isn't. Every time a fee is cut, three people get an education: the buyer, the seller and the broker. It is an education in exactly the wrong thing. You can't keep a buyer from knowing about a commission cut. When he learns of it he becomes trained as a commission-cutter. Better forget getting any listings from him; you'll never earn a full fee. The seller, of course, now has money to buy something but it won't profit you. He knows you as a weak sister and if, by accident, he deals with you, he'll work on your commission. He knows you cut them.

Saddest of all, however, is the education you get. When you cut a commission, you know you've lost. Nothing in the world can keep that knowledge from you, and you lose more than money. You lose your self-respect. You are unmasked, to yourself, as weak and ineffective. If you believe in the value of your services, a commission cut will eat you up and, eventually, drive you out of the business. It is too high a price to pay.

THE PARTIES

The Seller

Let's take a look at some of the situations we encounter with the seller. When you deal solely in exclusives, the problem of your commission seldom comes up during the listing process. When it does, however, it is usually broached in one of two forms:

1. The amount, or
2. How it is paid.

The discussion is always seller-initiated. There's no point in your bringing up the matter of commission; it's clearly stated in the listing. Typically, while reading the listing agreement prior to signing it, the seller will look up, with raised eyebrows, and say: "6%!"

It's your move. You have two options: Say nothing or reply. Both work. If you decide to say nothing, then say nothing. Don't even hiccup. Just sit there and look him in the eye. More than half the time the seller will drop his eyes and return to reading the listing.

If you wish to reply, just say: "That's correct, Mr. Roberts." Then, shut up. Don't defend it. Don't sell him. Just agree with him and be quiet. If the commission is really an issue with him, the seller will pursue it. If his comment ("6%!") was merely a standard ploy in the negotiating game, he will drop it when you show quiet strength.

"Net to Me"

Once in a while the seller will hit you with the "net to him" idea. On these occasions the seller is usually trying to assure himself of some net amount after paying you your commission. He may even wish to give you a net listing. Never take one. It always leads to hopeless confusion.

Everyone seems to know what "net" means when the listing is signed, but no one ever knows what it means when an offer is presented. Does "net" mean the amount the seller gets after deducting your commission? Or is it his proceeds after deducting all transaction costs such as title insurance, legal fees, insect infestation reports and work, recording fees, loan pay-off costs or other loan fees plus your commission? You can bet your life it will be the second view most of the time if you get in the habit of taking net listings.

Avoid the net listing problems altogether by not taking them. They are highly unprofessional and are often just a route to a commission cut taken by sophisticated sellers. The simplest way to handle this situation is to tell the seller: "I'm sorry, Mr. Roberts, but we don't take net listings; they lead to too much misunderstanding. Let's see if your price plus our fee is a sensible approach to the market. If it is, we'll take a listing at a price which includes our commission." Most sellers will go along with this approach. If they don't, leave the listing to someone else; it's a time waster.

5% or Six?

Another serious problem sometimes arises at the point of listing. This is the situation where a seller wants you to cut your commission rate. You charge 6%. He wants to pay 5%. There are several ways to handle this. One of them is to say: "Do you want 16% less service, Mr. Smith?"

Another approach that works is to explain that you are in sympathy with his desire, but a 5% rate would cut him off from the help of all cooperating brokers. Some men have also found this simple statement to have great power: "I'm sorry Mr. Smith, but I don't do that."

There is no excuse for listing at a cut commission. If you can't maintain your fee when you're listing the property, what are you going to do when there's a check lying on the table?

Secondary Financing

Some sellers are highly agreeable to carrying a second loan just so long as you get it as your commission. Such arrangements are fostered and perpetuated by brokers who pride themselves on taking their commission in kind. That is, they feel if they get the seller paper, they should be paid in paper. Such an idea is nonsense, pure stone-age thinking. It comes about because the sellers have "sold" the broker. How any seller can feel he has a broker who will fight for his seller's interests, when he won't even fight for his own vital interests, is beyond understanding. Think of the impression you make by being weak with the seller. Do you think sellers feel you can be weak with them but strong in dealing with a buyer? Not likely. List for a cash commission or you'll never see a cash commission.

Exchanges

Exchanges give rise to many nightmarish commission problems. These problems are the fault of the salesman who spends much of his time in a walking dream. A seller *might* be able to sell his property without you, but no seller will ever make a three-way exchange without you. If this be true, if your service is essential to a successful exchange, it follows that you should get paid in cash for your essential services. But many brokers settle for less. Why? I think it's because they don't fully understand their indispensable role in an exchange. And, sometimes, they force transactions that should never have been made in the first place. (For more on this problem take a look at Chapter 16.)

The Offer

At the offer stage a seller gets another shot at your commission. If anything, his attempts to cut you down at this point are even easier to control than they are at the listing level. If you've listed the property exclusively and shown by your every action that you expect full compensation in cash, you'll probably not have much trouble when you present your offer.

You may, however, have walked into a straight right hand when you listed it and not even have realized it. This is true of the listing that is priced just one commission away from a fair selling price. Let's say you took a listing at $110,000 which was really worth $103,000. A few weeks later you present a clean offer of $103,000. Your commission is $6180. What happens? Ever hear this? "Well, that's a fine offer, Sam. If I let it go for this, what are you going to do?"

What he means is, if I cut, how about you giving a little? Nice guy! Many brokers go along with him and they don't have to. The broker holds all the cards. He has a good offer and a check. All he has to do is play out his hand, refuse to cut his fee, and either get an acceptance or a counter-offer. All the pressure is on the seller.

If this happens to you, think about this: He wants to sell and I've got an offer. He has a 94% interest in the transaction, I have a 6% interest. If he refuses the offer, he still has the property and I still have the listing. What's wrong with that? That's where you came in; you haven't lost a thing. Leave the pressure where it ought to be—on the fellow with the 94% interest. Depart without an acceptance if you have to. He'll call you. And on your next listing, list it a little closer to market value.

Use the Counter-Offer

Here's another success technique to use on the commission-cutter. Just have him counter at a price which includes your full fee. The way to do this with full impact is to say: "Apparently I haven't done enough for you yet, Mr. Doe. Let's write a counter-offer at (say) $110,000. This includes a full fee to me. I'll go back and see if I can get the buyer to go that high." You might also remind the seller that, the moment he sets pen to paper and makes his counter-offer, he has destroyed the buyer's offer. It's a new ballgame. Some will take the chance, but not many. Chances are, if you use this idea, you'll sign off a good many offers without any counter-offer.

The Buyer

The value of listing them right is nowhere more apparent than dealing with a buyer. Many buyers are wise to the ways of the real estate world; they make all their offers just a commission away. They can't do this, of course, if the property is listed right. It would be taking too big a risk; they might lose the chance to buy it.

Get His Best "Shot"

To avoid a cut commission, get the buyer's best "shot" the first time. Fight for a good offer. After all, the higher your offer, the tougher it is for your seller to refuse it or counter it. He can't risk losing the sale either.

The Secret Price

All buyers (and sellers) have a secret price. If you want a full cash commission, work to uncover that secret price. Sometimes it's only another thousand dollars or two, but every little bit helps. Here's one way of getting it: "Mr. Brown, if when I present this offer we are only a thousand dollars apart, will you still buy this property?" The usual answer is "yes" or "of course." You reply, "Then give me that thousand right now so I can fight to get this property for you." You'll usually get it. Try this idea. Remember: that extra thousand may be part of your commission.

Some men have had success with this statement: "Give me a chance to buy this for you." This implies that the buyer's offer does not have much chance and unless he goes higher you're not going to be in his corner. It works, I think, because many buyers have the mistaken belief that you work solely for them.

Loan Costs

Some compromised commissions are inherent in the structure of the offer. This is certainly true in the case of the "one commission away" offer. Another common example of this problem is the offer that ignores loan costs. In this situation the buyer refuses to promise, in writing, to pay a definite sum to assume or obtain a loan. There are always costs involved in a loan, be it assumed or new, and if the offer is silent regarding these costs, guess who's going to pay them.

Here's some wording for your offer that will help you avoid this problem:

"Buyer will assume (or obtain) at his own expense not to exceed $_____ the existing (or a new) first loan in the approximate amount of $_____ payable at $_____ per month including _____% interest until paid. Any difference in the lender's statement (or the new loan amount) not to exceed $_____ will be adjusted in cash (or in the second)."

Check the wording with your attorney and make whatever adjustments local practice dictates. But use it. It will make you money.

Non-Cash Down Payments

Buyers without money cost you money. Few sellers will ever pay a cash commission out of a down payment that consists of second mortgages or diamonds or some other non-cash item. If you write transactions of this type, you'd better be mighty fond of second mortgages or diamonds because you're going to be up to your ears in them!

There is no need to consistently take property or paper for your fee. There is also no need to cut your fee. All that it takes to avoid paper, property or commission cuts is a strong, positive attitude on your part. Remember this: Once you start to cut, there is no bottom. Once the seller draws your commission blood, he won't be content until he plays in it.

When you get a full cash commission, you win. To win you've got to be willing to lose. That is, you've got to be willing to put it all on the line and, occasionally, walk out with no sale. Peculiar thing though—it never happens. I've seen thousands of transactions and I've yet to meet the first seller who would kill a transaction over a commission.

POINTS TO REMEMBER

—Cash commissions start with your listing.
—Cut commissions are a disservice to your profession.
—If you assume you'll be paid a full cash commission; you will be.
—Half a loaf is not better than none.
—Cutting a commission educates buyer, broker, and seller in the wrong thing.
—Avoid net listings.
—There is no excuse for listing at a cut commission.
—Exchanges often set up commission cutting.
—If your services are worth anything they are worth what you ask.
—Overpriced listings help the seller to bargain with you over your fee.
—In a commission game you hold all the best cards.
—In a typical transaction the seller has a 94% interest, you have a 6% interest.
—Leave the pressure where it belongs.
—Use the counter offer to solve a commission problem.
—When you list property right buyers can't chance low offers.
—Dig for the secret price.
—Use "Give me a chance to buy this for you."
—Don't avoid financing costs in your offer.
—Avoid non-cash down payments.
—You'll never win a commission battle unless you're willing to lose.

14

Costly Mistakes to Avoid

It has been said that experience is the best teacher. Whether this be true or not, one thing is certain: Experience is the most expensive teacher! The school of hard knocks is always open; it accepts anyone.

The mistakes discussed in this chapter cost the salesmen who made them well over one million dollars. Perhaps you've already paid the price to learn some of these things. If so, welcome to the club. If not, you have a rare opportunity to be one of those who profits from the experiences of others.

The Biggest Mistake

The biggest, most costly mistake of them all is the non-exclusive listing. The practice of taking open listings has cost brokers an untold amount of money. In thousands of cases it has cost the broker his entire business.

Open listings breed incompetence. Many salesmen look for the easy way out. That way appears to be the open listing. Because anyone will sign an "open," it is not necessary to get good at your business to take one. The newest man in our business can be taught in one hour how to take an open listing. In one week he can have listings on everything in sight.

The Easy Way

"Opens," however, are not really the easy way to go. Most open-listed owners have no confidence in you or your firm. Many such listings are incomplete, inaccurate or both. Because client confidence is lacking and the property information is inadequate, the broker's job is hard, not easy.

You Must Do 100% of the Work

The process of getting a listing and making a sale can never exceed 100% of the work required. The only real question is, when do you do the work? It might be thought of in this way:

	Open Listing	Exclusive Listing
Listing Effort	10%	50%
Sales Effort	90%	50%
Total Effort	100%	100%

You are eventually going to have to do all the work necessary to get a sale. Why not divide it equally between listing and selling? Success-program salesmen do.

Head-in-the-Sand Errors

Here's a story which illustrates an error that belongs in a big group of errors. I call them the head-in-the-sand type because they never occur unless the broker tries to hide from them.

A sale of $400,000 was made. The negotiations had been delicate and complicated; they extended over three weeks. Many offers and counter-offers had been negotiated and renegotiated. Agreement was finally reached. A $24,000 commission was in sight. Most of the negotiating difficulty had been with the sellers. When they signed the final acceptance, however, they seemed happy. They weren't. . . .

The Escrow

In our area the closing details are handled by an escrow arrangement. That is, each party to the transaction instructs the escrow holder (a neutral party) to carry out the details necessary to transfer title pursuant to the agreement between buyer and seller. It is customary for the broker (who is not a party to the escrow) to dictate necessary escrow instructions and get these instructions signed by the buyer and seller. Escrow also draws all notes and grant deeds and receives miscellaneous documents such as the personal property inventory or lease assignments. So much for the background. Here's the head-in-the-sand error.

Get All Necessary Signatures Promptly

When buyer and seller have documents to sign get them signed all at once. Don't do it in stages. In the above transaction the seller had to sign escrow instructions, a grant deed, a personal property inventory and an authorization for an insect infestation report. The salesman had them sign their escrow instructions within 36 hours of their acceptance of the offer. He then buried his head in the sand and put off for three weeks asking for their signature on the grant deed and other documents. He never got it. A $400,000 sale ($24,000 commission) went out the window because the salesman failed to obey this cardinal rule: *If there are papers to sign, get them signed all at once.* In the three weeks that intervened between the signing of the escrow instructions and the request to sign the other documents, the seller decided not to sell. He was determined to frustrate the sale by refusing to cooperate.

This sale would have closed if the salesman had been a good mechanic and gotten all documents signed at once. It would have closed had the salesman faced his problems squarely and promptly. It is impossible to believe the salesman did not know of the seller's unhappiness with the transaction. Surely sometime during the three weeks of inactivity the seller gave some sign of discontent. Yet the salesman acted as if the problem didn't exist; he buried his head and hoped the problems would go away. They never do. Every time you bury your head in the sand you'll get kicked in the rear. Chalk up a $24,000 lesson—twice the cost of a good college education.

The Disappearing Salesman

There is another group of expensive mistakes closely akin to the preceding example. It is called the disappearing salesman error. In this type of error the salesman faces a problem (it can be big or small) which he knows will upset his sale. Does he come to grips with it? No. He disappears; no one can find him; he thinks the problem will go away or solve itself. It seldom happens. What usually happens is the problem gets bigger and the sale blows.

I once saw a million dollar sale go up in smoke because of this. The buyer tried for three days to reach the salesman by telephone. Every telephone message sent the salesman into a paroxism of fear. He smelled trouble. He didn't answer any of them. All the buyer wanted was a more exact legal description. But by the time the salesman overcame his fear and called the buyer, it was too late. The buyer was so infuriated by the lack of service that he killed the transaction. A $50,000 learning experience!

Once you get them signed off, stick around. Don't run away and hide. All transactions have problems but most problems are small. When you ignore trouble it gets worse, it seldom becomes less. Don't be a coward; face up to every situation and deal with it quickly. The worst that can happen is losing the sale. You'll lose it anyway if you ignore the problems.

Leases

In commercial property the obligations of the tenant and the responsibilities of the landlord are spelled out in the lease. This document controls the income and, to a large degree, the expense connected with the property. When listing commercial property, you must get a copy of the leases—without them you're lost.

More sales are lost because of inaccurate information or a lack of information than for any other single reason. In commercial property almost all information problems stem from the lease.

Here's an expensive example: we listed four stores in a major shopping center for $185,000. The gross annual income was $23,400. The net income was $19,320 and the property showed approximately 10.4% return on the sales price. The landlord was responsible for parking lot maintenance. He included $600 per year in the income which, he claimed, was an amount paid to him by the tenants in excess of the cost of parking lot maintenance. The tenants, it appeared, were obligated to pay a flat sum per month for parking lot maintenance rather than the more usual pro-rata share of actual expense.

The property was sold for $185,000 subject to the buyer's right to disapprove the leases, in writing, within 48 hours. He disapproved them. There was no provision in the leases for the tenants' flat-sum payment. The leases, in fact, stated each tenant was to pay his pro-rata share of the actual cost of parking lot maintenance.

This sale was lost because the income was misrepresented. The income was misrepresented because the listing salesman never read the leases. An $11,100 commission was sacrificed on the altar of incompetency.

Options

Leases often contain option-to-purchase clauses or a first right of refusal provision. Both can be a deadly trap for the careless salesman.

They can both cost you your commission. A $15,000 commission was lost in the following case: a gas station was listed on a non-exclusive basis. The price was $250,000. It was sold in a week. Up popped the tenant's right to match any bona fide offer (a first right of refusal). The tenant bought the station for $250,000. The broker got no commission. Reason: the broker had not read the lease and he did not have an exclusive. The seller was free to accept the tenant's purchase and pay the broker nothing, which he did. The broker lost a $250,000 sale and a $15,000 commission because he forgot to get a copy of the lease and read it.

Even string store leases to momma and poppa tenants can cause you difficulties. In a group of eight stores which sold recently, the salesman took the seller's word that all tenants had a lease. They didn't. The seller was not trying to deliberately deceive his broker; he really believed he had a lease with all his tenants. But the seller hadn't reviewed the situation recently. He was speaking from memory. And he was wrong. The biggest tenant's lease had expired many months before the sale. The new owner, of course, discovered this during the closing procedure, when it became apparent that the lease being assigned to him had expired. Fortunately this sale was saved since the salesman was able to negotiate a new lease with the tenant. But the salesman had to do this leasing work free of charge in order to save his sale and his reputation. All this difficulty and confusion could have been avoided had the listing salesman (or his broker) *insisted* upon having a copy of the leases and had read them.

Get Copies of All Leases

Most of your lease problems can be avoided if you will get a copy of *each* lease at the time of listing and if you'll read those leases *before* you try to sell the property to anyone. You might develop a lease checklist such as the following:

LEASE ABSTRACT CHECK SHEET

Property address _____ City _____

Parties
Tenants _____ If tenant a corporation, does anyone have personal liability on this lease? Yes ____ No ____. If yes, who? _____

Terms of Lease
Starting date _____ Ending date _____. Cancellation clauses Yes ____ No ____. If yes, explain _____

Lease options: Yes _____ No _____. If yes, explain monthly rental, etc.

Rental Payments

Monthly rental $_____ Due date _____ Security deposit
$_____ Last months rent _____. Percentage or gallonage clause.
Yes _____ No _____. Explain: How calculated? When payable: Monthly,
quarterly, yearly? Is it adjusted quarterly, monthly? Recapture: Does
tenant have right to recapture *any* expense out of percentage or gallonage
rent? How? _____

Rent escalator clause: (Cost of living, etc.) Yes _____ No _____. Explain:
Amount? How? When? _____

Expenses

Taxes: Tenant pays all, none, pro rata share, etc. How? When? Base year?
Amount? _____
Insurance: Who pays? Fire, liability, plate glass, minimum coverage re-
quired by lease: _____
Interior maintenance _____
Exterior maintenance _____
Common area parking _____
Lighting: Parking lot & exterior _____
Utilities: Who pays? Separate meters? _____
Other expenses: Janitor Service, etc. _____
Air conditioning: Who pays maintenance? _____

Alterations, Remodeling, Fixturization

Can tenant make any structural changes? _____
Who pays for improvements desired by tenant? _____
Who owns tenant-installed improvements? _____
Who provided the trade fixtures? _____
Is there a monthly payment on trade fixtures? How much? Does it affect
percentage rent? _____

Assignment

Can this lease be assigned? Yes _____ No _____. Will tenant have any con-
tinuing responsibility if he assigns the lease or sublets? _____.
Are there any limitations or restrictions on the use of the leased property?

Sub Lease? Yes _____ No _____. If yes, explain: _____

Amendments

Has this lease been amended? Yes _____ No _____. If yes, explain _____

Other Information

First right of refusal? Yes _____ No _____. If yes, Explain: Number of days, etc. _____

Option to purchase? Yes _____ No _____. If yes, explain: _____

Lease recorded? Yes _____ No _____. If yes, subordination clause, etc. _____

Do you have a copy of the lease? Yes _____ No _____. If yes, where? _____

To use this form simply read the lease and fill in the answer to each question as you run across it in the lease. Here's a time-saving trick: Each time you find the answer to one of the questions in the checklist, enter both the answer and page number of the lease where you found that answer. It will save you many hours of time later when you sit down with the buyer or his attorney to review the leases.

Cancellation Clauses

Avoid any listing with a cancellation clause. Such listings are a waste of time. They will usually cost you money. Sellers who insist upon the right to cancel a listing after 60 or 90 days are not sold on you or your services. They want to hedge their bet and, often, they want to be in position to compete with you in your search for a buyer. They're fierce competitors because they have a monetary advantage; their price is five or six percent less than yours.

If you are active in your pursuit of a buyer, 80–90% of your listings with a cancellation clause will be cancelled. You will stir up such a commotion among the qualified buyers that one or two of them will certainly check directly with the owner. When they do, it's all over. The buyer and the seller will outwait you. The seller will cancel and negotiate his own sale. Client registration doesn't help. Such buyers have more buying names than there are grains of sand on the beach.

A cancellation provision in an exclusive listing makes that listing very much like an "open."

The Cancellation Request

Most well-written exclusives are irrevocable. Occasionally, however, a client will want to cancel an exclusive listing. Don't do it.

Most cancellation requests are accompanied by loud noises from the seller and many exaggerated statements alleging broker error. It's all smoke.

Clients request cancellation to make their own sale without having to pay a commission. This is true in nine times out of every ten cancellation requests. If you are a patsy and agree to cancel you'll give up millions of dollars worth of business. Leave the pressure on the seller; let him cancel and risk a judgment if he wants to.

The Answer

Always respond to a cancellation request with an offer to release the property from showing. The release from showing suspends all sales activity but it does not cancel the listing. It is the perfect answer for the client who has honestly decided not to sell. It removes the property from the market but does not change the seller's obligation for a commission should he sell it himself during the term of your listing.

The release from showing should be a specially printed form, rather than an informal typewritten document.

Deferred Commissions

Leases often give rise to commissions payable over long periods. Many brokers have lost money by their failure to get the commission payment arrangements in writing.

Here's an idea for you. If your lease commission is payable over a time period exceeding one year, get a written agreement that the entire unpaid balance becomes immediately due and payable, at your option, if the property is sold or conveyed in any way. Failure to cover this problem puts the old landlord in the position of paying for a dead horse. Most won't do it.

POINTS TO REMEMBER

—The biggest mistake of all is the non-exclusive listing.
—Open listings breed incompetence.
—To get a sale you must do 100% of the work.
—Don't bury your head in the sand. Solve your problems while they're small.
—Get all signatures promptly.
—Don't play hard to get.
—Get a copy of all leases.
—Use the lease abstract check list.
—Purchase options can cost you a commission.
—Use the release from showing device.
—Accelerate all deferred commissions.

15

Overcoming Objections
That Kill Sales

How many times have you seen a transaction stopped dead by a devastating statement of some disadvantage? It happens constantly, in both listing and selling situations. Quite often the sale-killing disadvantage is of a common variety; it ought not to pack such a lethal punch. Why then, do these ordinary, oft-repeated disadvantages continue to upset transactions? They don't. The man on the success-program stopped losing sales to common objections long ago.

There is a basic truth about the investment world: *There is no such thing as a perfect investment.* Success-program brokers know this. So do all the buyers and all the sellers.

Knowing that no perfect real estate investment vehicle has ever been created, the success-program salesman can look at every investment opportunity from all sides. He is objective. He is not thrown offstride by the disadvantages present in a transaction. There are disadvantages in every transaction.

Cash It In

What can you do with this truth? Briefly, *Don't avoid the disadvantages—cash them in.* Consider this for a moment: The customers who voice routine disadvantages know, just as you do, that other investment forms have disadvantages too; many of them bigger than any disadvantage ever found in income real estate. You might also find it interesting to think of this: if clients know of these disadvantages (and they do), why are they talking to you? Could it be that they've weighed the advantages and disadvantages and the scale tipped to the advantages? Many customers mouth disadvantages just as other people say "it's a nice day." It's just idle conversation designed to fill up moments when nothing of importance is being said.

FIXED INCOME INVESTMENTS

Any property leased for long periods without a change in income is a fixed income investment. Such properties are often leased for as much as 20 years to AAA credits (sometimes called corporate signatures) and are often referred to as "well-leased."

The Disadvantage

How can a 20 year lease with a tenant like Standard Oil be bad? Because long leases without any change in income are as bad as holding cash in a bank. Inflation eats you up. You can do nothing about it. Your property may rise in value but you are unable to realize this value through a sale because your income reflects a much lower value. You are "locked-in" for the period of your lease. The problem is worsened when a rise in yields occurs along with inflation.

The Answer

Is there an answer to this problem? Here are five parts of the answer. Perhaps these will suggest other approaches to you.

First, one can only buy and sell in today's market. We can't buy at yesterday's prices and sell at tomorrow's. We must make our decisions now.

Second, your cash return, once achieved, never changes. You always get what you bargained for.

Third, most fixed income investments are created by their holders. They are not often sold to second or third parties. The holder then ought to protect himself with rent escalation provisions. Percentage rents and gallonage clauses often try to do this job.

Fourth, the leases ought to contain (and normally do) tax protection and other expense protection clauses.

Fifth, you often hear about the vacancy problem in commercial property. You won't have one here for 20 years. It is not unusual, however, to hear: "When you have a vacancy in this property it will last a long time." True. Think of this: long vacancies = long occupancies.

FLEXIBLE INCOME INVESTMENTS

Any property where the tenancy is month-to-month, or where leases do not exceed one year, is a flexible income property. The apartment house is the usual example.

The Disadvantage

Income from such property tends to fall quickly in a declining market. The income is very sensitive to economic change. Month-to-month tenancies are generally weak credits (sometimes called personal signatures). They are highly speculative investments.

The Answer

Make sure your customer is psychologically suited to this type of investment, if he is, point out that:

—The speculative nature of month-to-month tenants puts the owner in a highly flexible position.

—In a rising market the landlord may levy an immediate rent increase. He may continue with rent increases every three or four months, if needed, to keep abreast of the market. In the worst market we've ever seen, good property (that was well maintained) suffered very little vacancy.

—While rents may have to be lowered (try "adjusted") during a poor market, you are able to respond at once as soon as conditions improve. Point out examples of this from your own experience.

CHARACTERISTIC DISADVANTAGES

Income property by its very nature has some built-in disadvantages. Among these are:

        —Management
        —Liquidity
        —Equity build up vs spendable income
        —Furnish vs unfurnished rentals

Management

We often hear "I don't buy real estate because there is too much management." That's a lot of baloney! Every investment has management problems. Think of stocks and bonds for a moment. No management? Relatively little management? What *is* a little management?

Did the people jumping out of windows in 1929 feel that stocks required little or no management? Ever watch a serious security investor? Try it sometime. Drop into your local stock broker's office at the opening of market for seven days running. You don't know what management problems are until you've seen the maneuvers of the stock buyer in a down market. A call from a tenant complaining of a stopped up drain will seem like a pleasure compared to a margin call from your broker.

Here's another approach to the management objection. It is philosophical. These ideas will suggest other answers to you. "When did it happen, in America, that we began to expect something for nothing? Everything worth having involves work. There is a price on every success. The price you pay to succeed as an owner of real estate is your ability to manage well. About the only significant difference between a successful business and one that is unsuccessful is the quality of management. Why would you want to remove your unique talents from this investment?"

Liquidity

"Real estate is not liquid. I can't get my cash out of it in a hurry." Not so. I've seen major properties sold in less than four hours.

Or, how about this one: "When you buy real estate you turn cash into paper. That is, when you go to sell, you can't get your cash out; you get a second mortgage."

Try these answers. First, real estate is as liquid as the price in the mind of the seller. Why can you sell stock so fast? Stock is sold in an auction market. The seller takes the *going* price or he keeps it. There is seldom a negotiated price.

When real estate is offered at a "fair" price, it sells fast. It is often only the desire of sellers to maximize their price that slows down the sale. Unhurried sellers often get a premium price this way. Most sellers could get a quick sale by simply pricing at the *going* rate.

Is it hard to cash out? Yes and no. Most well-bought properties will return your original cash investment on a sale. The "paper" is usually the profit.

Many salesmen have found it easy to get sellers to carry second mortgages by saying: "Why don't you sell this and start earning interest on your equity?" Many sellers have no idea what they will do with their equity even if they get it in cash. The idea of earning interest on it is quite appealing.

Equity Build-up Vs. Spendable Income

Does this sound familiar? "Don't talk to me about equity build-up. All properties have equity build-up. Tell me about the spendable." Here are three ideas for you.

First, maneuver the customer into saying something like "I can earn more return than that by putting my money in the bank." Then try this answer: "Yes that's true. However (not "but") you will *never* own the bank." Such an answer points out, dramatically, the real value of equity build-up.

Second, try this. Ask your customer what he thinks he is paying for the property. Let's say it is $100,000 with $10,000 down. He is going to say $100,000. You can ask "Isn't it really $10,000? If you are buying this right all you'll ever pay for it is $10,000. The tenants will pay the rest."

Third, think of equity and spendable as opposite ends of the same string. When you pull on one end the other has got to move. When equity build-up goes down (by lower payments) spendable goes up. Some see the idea as a teeter-totter with equity build-up on one side and spendable income on the other.

The point is this, no one can talk of one without recognizing the other. Any customer who wants you to ignore equity build-up is kidding both himself and you. They are forever linked.

Furnished Vs. Unfurnished Rentals

Many investors have lost good investments because of their prejudiced attitude toward furniture.

Furniture, the objection goes, causes you to attract a lower class of tenant and to experience a high turnover. Maintenance, it is claimed, is increased due to the turnover. Sounds right. Actual operating experience, however, indicates a little better profit experience than the objection seems to acknowledge.

Here are some ideas you can use to develop a good answer to this objection. First, the dollar return on a furniture investment far exceeds the return earned on the real estate. Second, the depreciation permitted is faster than the actual loss of the asset; this increases your return. Add to this the idea that most "hard" pieces (end table, coffee tables, lamps, etc.) do not have to be replaced every five years and you can paint a very bright dollar-return figure.

Maintenance, to the average buyer, usually means painting and replacing carpet. This is especially true when it is raised as an objection in connection with furnished rentals. Those who operate thousands of furnished rentals tell us that the tenants are not as demanding as unfurnished rental tenants. The units need not be repainted on each move out. The tenant will put up with slightly worn carpet. Operating experience shows that such maintenance expenses do not exceed that found in unfurnished rentals.

Tenants turnover is an interesting objection. A quick answer involves pointing out that furnished rentals rent faster than unfurnished. Overall rent loss to vacancy is often much less in furnished units.

POINTS TO REMEMBER

—Garden-variety objections ought not kill a sale.
—There is no perfect investment.
—Don't avoid common objections—cash them in.
—Your customers know the facts of investment life.
—Many objections are just conversation fillers.
—One must buy and sell at *today's* price.
—Long vacancies = long occupancy.
—A client ought to be psychologically suited to an investment.
—With month-to-month rents you can raise your income quickly.
—All investments require management.
—Real estate is as liquid as is the price in the mind of the seller.
—A sale often puts the seller in the position of earning interest on his equity.
—Equity build-up and spendable income are forever linked.
—Furnished rentals can be a better investment than unfurnished.

16

Profitable Exchanging

Exchanging makes sense but many exchangors don't. Exchanging solves some real economic problems for many equity owners. It can create a multitude of economic problems for brokers who don't approach this service in a business-like way. The market for exchange service is much bigger than most of us can imagine. This market has been unnecessarily restricted by unsound practices. Exchanging is held in low repute by many qualified brokers, clients, and lenders. These parties have been made wary of exchanges due to excesses in pricing and the unrealistic approaches and unbusinesslike practices often found in exchanges. Exchanging has far too often been the exchange of one disappointment for another. No one really wants it that way, but that is the way it often turns out, due mainly to the unrealistic attitude of the first party to the exchange.

The Measure of Success

An exchange must make economic sense to all parties to be considered a success. Many brokers define a successful exchange as one that closes. This seems to be a rather limited definition. A truly successful exchange not only closes, but the broker who arranges it receives a full cash commission from both sides. Most exchanges you hear about will not pass this more strenuous test of success.

Your Commission

All too often the broker receives less than a full-cash commission. Sometimes he takes "paper" as his fee. Or, worse still, he ends up owning one of the smaller properties. Such ownership implies a sale sometime in the future. The broker then becomes a principal. Many brokers do not enjoy being cast in the principal's role. They are jealous of their independent, third-party status and will go to any length to protect it even to the length of avoiding exchanges. This view, of course, does not preclude the very sound practice of a broker making long-term investments for his own account.

When a broker receives less than a full-cash commission the best interest of the broker and his clients is not served. Any time you are tempted to accept something other than full cash for your services ask yourself this: "If what I am doing is worth anything, how come I can't get paid for it?"

Selfish Interests

One of the most intriguing aspects of exchanging is that all parties to the exchange have their own unique, selfish interests. Yet, in a successful exchange, these legitimate selfish interests coincide and are mutually beneficial. For example: The broker wants and needs a full-cash commission from both sides. At first glance the other parties might feel this apparently selfish desire of the broker places too much of a burden on them. In thinking it through, however, it seems logically to benefit everyone.

If brokers do not receive a full-cash commission for their services, they won't be able to continue in business. Any compensation other than full-cash confuses the broker's role and discourages those best able to serve from entering or staying in the field. If the success-program for exchanges is followed, it benefits all parties to the exchange; deviating from it generally means wasting time, losing client confidence, and failure to make a trade.

The Parties to an Exchange

There are usually four important parties to an average exchange.

Party #1—He initiates the exchange. He owns the smaller property.

Party #2—He has what Party #1 wants.

Party #3—The "cash-out" buyer. He has what Party #2 wants —CASH. Truly the indispensable man. He acquires property #1 from Party #2.

Party #4—The broker—he has what all the other parties need —the talent, the inventory, the facilities.

Such a classification eliminates the two-party exchange. These are extremely rare. So rare, in fact, that one speaker was led to say: "There ain't no such thing as a two-way exchange."

The Success Program for Exchanging

Here are the essential elements of the success-pattern:

One, work with smaller properties as property #1. Properties valued between $25,000 and $100,000 are ideal.

Two, use high-equity properties as property #1. A free and clear situation is good. More than one loan on property #1 is a failure signal.

Three, price property #1 at its true market value. It may be argued that a price slightly below market is in the best interest of party #1.

Four, have a full term (or at least six months) exclusive on all properties involved in the exchange. This must be a "for sale" listing, not a "for trade" listing.

Five, explain the exchange process fully to party #1 with special emphasis on the role of party #3—the "cash-out" buyer. Eventually, of course, party #2 is going to have to understand the function of the "cash-out" buyer also.

Six, work with properties you know in areas you know. All elements of this success-program are essential. If one of them is missing or is compromised the chance of success is considerably weakened.

The First Property

The first property is the critical ingredient. There are two essential elements: size and equity. Working with smaller properties as property #1 is important. These owners need your service. It is easier to "cash-out" a smaller property because the market is more active and much broader.

A free and clear or high-equity property is essential. Quite often, to facilitate a sale to the third party, it will be necessary for the first party to carry back a small part of the purchase price as a first or second loan. This reduces the effective equity available for trade but it is so often necessary that it should not be ignored. The existence of a high equity also makes cash generation, through new loans, possible. Cash is of interest to the second party and to you.

Pricing

The pricing of the first property is also critical. Most of the time you are going to need a third party, as a buyer of the first property, to make the exchange feasible. You can't afford to look for a buyer if the property is not a good value. There is another value in pricing the first property properly: When property #1 is priced right, it follows that property #2 will enter the exchange at the right price. Party #1 will see to that.

Proper pricing is also essential to attract loans. Most lenders are wary of lending on values "created" in the typical exchange. Consequently, financing is made unnecessarily difficult. It need not be so. The existence of a cash buyer for property #1 considerably increases the confidence of the lender in the integrity of the entire transaction. Improper pricing is a failure signal. It is generally true that *if it won't sell it won't trade.*

There Is a Risk

Every business venture has an element of risk. In the success-program for exchanging, the risk is that the first party might not be able to effect an exchange. To find a "cash-out" buyer you must have full-term, "for sale" exclusive authorization. If the "cash-out" buyer is located before an exchange property is found, this buyer must know (even though he has to wait) that he will get the property someday. Typically, the agreement with the "cash-out" buyer provides for a 90 to 120 day closing time to allow the seller to find a suitable exchange property. It may also provide, among other things, for the buyer to take title from an as-yet-unknown seller. In the event no suitable exchange property is found within the time allowed, the seller (Party #1) agrees to make a normal sale to the "cash-out" buyer. The seller will then have a capital gain tax to pay. But is this really a disaster? The tax is always due. Exchanging only defers it.

Many thinkers on this subject feel that the time to pay a tax is when you incur it and have the money to pay it. In many cases more money has been lost trying to avoid taxes, by acquiring over-priced exchange properties, than would have been lost by paying the tax in the first place. If you work with smaller properties the tax, in event of sale, will seldom be large enough to break your client. Not all exchanges are tax-oriented, of course. They don't have to be.

But tax considerations are probably the single most important motivation for an exchange. When this motivation is absent you should strenuously question the reason for exchanging.

Importance of "Cash-Out" Buyer

The risk of paying the tax seems worth it from another point of view. With a "cash-out" buyer on tap, the first party approaches all properties virtually as a cash buyer. He comes bearing cash, not property. This strengthens his position as a buyer and virtually assures a proper price for the property he acquires.

Price, Selection

The use of the "cash-out" buyer also makes practically all properties available to the first party. Most properties are offered for sale; few are offered on an exchange only basis; especially on an exchange-down basis. The broader selection available will often convince party number one that the "risk" of paying a tax is a reasonable one.

You Must Have an Exclusive

The need for an exclusive listing is a self-evident truth. Nothing spells confidence like an exclusive. It takes time to make a favorable exchange. An exclusive gives you time.

The lack of an exclusive listing is a failure signal that can't be ignored. This lack dooms more potential exchanges than any other single weakness. A seller who tries to work an exchange without giving an exclusive to a competent broker fools only himself. No one can give his full attention to someone who hasn't placed his complete confidence in the broker.

All Parties Must Understand

Poor communication between the parties to an exchange often shatters the success-program. All parties must have a full understanding of the exchange process. To reach this understanding with Party #1 could take several hours of discussion and explanation. Failure to spend an adequate amount of time in this area will result in delays in the transaction at critical times. To acquire the best properties often requires quick, decisive action on the part of Party #1. Incomplete understanding of the exchange process makes fast action impossible.

Work in Your Own Backyard

In exchanging, knowledge is power. It is next to impossible to properly advise clients who seek to sell or acquire out-of-area properties. You usually don't know the property or the area and you can seldom afford the time investment required to get even minimum knowledge. When you get out of your own backyard, the failure signal bell is ringing loud and clear. Even if you should make such a transaction, the time, money, and energy you will spend doing it could probably be more profitably employed close to home. It is difficult to see how one builds a local reputation selling property in a town 500 or 1000 miles away.

Service and Earnings

A great opportunity for service and earnings exists in properly handled exchanges. Many qualified brokers already provide this service. Such brokers appear to be alert for failure signals. They take immediate corrective action when they appear. They work with properly priced properties, which are under their full control, and with people who understand the entire exchange process. And they earn full cash commissions. Any broker who follows the success-program, and has a thorough knowledge of income property can do it.

POINTS TO REMEMBER

—Exchanging may be the answer to some tax problems.
—The need for exchange service is bigger than most of us imagine.
—The market for exchange service has been narrowed by the unsound practices of some unqualified exchangors.
—Exchanging is often the exchange of one disappointment for another.
—An exchange must make economic sense to all parties.
—An exchange is a success when the broker gets cash as his commission.
—Accepting property as your commission may make it difficult to maintain your neutral, third party role.
—If a service is worth anything people will pay for it in cash.
—There are four essential parties to the success pattern exchange.
—When you try to "beat" the success pattern you get more experience than money.
—All elements of the success pattern are essential.
—Work with small properties.
—Work with high equity properties.
—If it won't sell, it won't trade.
—Price the first property right.
—Proper pricing makes getting loans easier.
—Every business venture contains some risk.
—The three-way exchange method is not foolproof.
—The "cash-out" buyer must know he is going to get title eventually.

—Not all exchanges are tax motivated.

—Exchanging is not the only answer to a real estate tax problem.

—It is often wise to pay the tax when you have the money to pay it.

—More money has been lost trying to avoid taxes by making hasty, unprofitable exchanges, than has been deferred by exchanges.

—By using a three-way exchange party number one enters the market as a cash buyer.

—To make a profitable exchange you must have time and control; an exclusive gives you both.

—Poor communication dooms many exchanges.

—Work in your own backyard.

—Exchanging offers an opportunity for service and earnings.

17

Working with Other Professionals

You don't function in a vacuum. To achieve maximum success you must have the goodwill and active cooperation of many other professionals. In this chapter you'll find money-making ideas on how to work with attorneys, accountants, fellow brokers, and lenders. All of the people in these groups can send you more business than you can handle. But to get their referrals you must know how to work with them.

ATTORNEYS

Attorneys are a fact of business life. Only the amateur or the incompetent fears their influence or seeks to avoid them. The real pro enjoys working with attorneys and advises his clients to seek their help.

Complicated Negotiations

Attorneys will help you make more transactions than they will ever kill. This is true of all types of transactions, but is especially true of the bigger, more complicated negotiations.

If you are working on build-to-suit or ground lease transactions, you'd better be adept at working with attorneys because it is impossible to complete such negotiations without their expert assistance. Several of our recent major discount store transactions (all of which were build-to-suit or ground leases) went together largely because of the expertise of the attorneys involved and because of the confidence the principals placed in their attorneys. Such transactions are complicated. They are always full of unexpected legal problems. These problems can cause the principals to take hasty, ill-considered action. At such times the attorneys are often the only ones able to restore the calm and reasoning approach necessary to conclude the transaction.

Success Techniques

It is always easier to get along with someone if your relationship starts off right. The first rule for dealing successfully with attorneys is: *Write all the documents as if they were going to be reviewed by an attorney*. Even if you know there is no attorney in the picture, you owe it to your client to prepare your listing agreement, offer to purchase or proposal to lease as if there were. It's a professional habit that will pay big dividends.

Quite often a client will seek legal advice without your knowledge. If you become involved with a client's attorney, you won't start with two strikes against you if you've followed good procedure in the preparation of all documents. It's always comforting to know that all of your documents are professionally done. Remember, while attorneys are protecting buyers and sellers, they automatically protect you.

When an attorney is engaged, arrange to meet him. Go with your client and be available to answer questions when he sees his attorney. Many transactions are lost because of poor communication between the broker and the client's attorney. The ineffective communication is seldom the attorney's fault.

Treat the attorney like your client. If he represents the seller, treat him like the seller. If he is the buyer's attorney treat him like the buyer. Assume that the business deal is made and that his role is that of attending to the legal arrangements. But, be careful with this assumption. Many clients who use an attorney have a long-standing, extremely close relationship with their attorney. He's the one who has drawn their will, organized their business, or handled their divorce. The relationship has stood the test of time. Don't fight it. Work with it.

Respect an attorney's time. Many brokers are discourteous in this matter. They seem to forget that the attorney, like us, has two things to offer: time and talent. It is surprising how many times I hear complaints from fine attorneys about brokers who storm into their office without an appointment, demanding immediate attention. Don't do this. If you do you'll be on a failure course and attorneys will always be difficult to work with.

Keep the attorney informed. When a client retains an attorney, make up your mind to cooperate with that attorney. Check with him by telephone before asking the client to make a decision. Review any written agreements with him. Send him copies of everything.

Difficult Attorneys

Every human activity is plagued by difficult people. The law is no exception. Once in a while you may run across an attorney who seems to have majored in arrogance and minored in sarcasm in college. Such attorneys are a rarity. But when you get involved with one, you'll find meaningful communication is impossible.

In such cases, relax. Be courteous, be brief, avoid argument. Return to your buyer or seller and explain to him that virtually no basis exists for intelligent communication between you and the attorney. Explain that, in this very rare situation, you have found it practical for the client to consult privately with his attorney and then meet with you. Never, never criticize the attorney. Your criticism will probably be unjust. It will always hurt you, not the attorney.

Attorneys can be a powerful source of referral business. Remember: Buyers are sellers and sellers are buyers. Every attorney you deal with is representing a buyer or a seller. He will diligently pursue the interests of his client. If you vigorously represent your client's interest with objectivity and honesty you'll score high with most attorneys. With the right attitude on your part and with a fair transaction in hand you'll find 99 out of 100 attorneys are both helpful and important to your transaction.

ACCOUNTANTS

Your involvement with accountants will seldom be as extensive as your exposure to attorneys. But as tax considerations become increasingly important in real estate transactions, you'll find more occasion to confer with the accountant of either buyer or seller.

Be Prepared

Much of the difficulty inexperienced salesmen have in dealing with either attorneys or accountants stems from the salesman's lack of knowledge. To put it candidly: The salesman doesn't know what he's talking about. This generates fear and from this fear comes the desire to avoid a confrontation with the expert knowledge of the buyer's or seller's other advisors. Fear makes you weak. You can never negotiate from weakness.

The only way you'll ever be able to work with an accountant with confidence is to arm yourself with enough information to make it possible to carry on a meaningful conversation. In short, get smart. Get educated. Study basic accounting. Take some tax courses. Enroll in an exchange course. Don't try to become an accountant or a tax expert, but get familiar enough with the problems to understand them and to discuss them.

Assuming you have the educational background, you must prepare yourself for the particular interview. Accountants live with figures. Here's your chance to use your beautiful projections. No sale is ever made solely on the basis of the numbers. If the numbers are ever going to be important, however, it's now.

Be accurate. Double check every calculation. Nothing destroys you faster than simple mathematical errors. Don't depend upon yourself to make all the calculations required. Get yourself a tape calculator.

Be organized. Present your data on a spread sheet or in some other logical fashion. Get rid of all those scratch pad and back-of-envelope calculations that you used with the buyer or seller.

Respect his time. Just as with attorneys, time is money. Don't waste it. Don't be demanding.

Difficult Accountants

Here's an idea that will smooth the road if it gets too rough. You can also use this, occasionally, to solve the difficult attorney problem: Have one accountant talk to another. Many of our communication problems with accountants come from a vocabulary problem; we don't talk their language. Often you can solve this problem by having your company CPA discuss the accounting problems with the accountant who seems to be causing problems.

In leasing and build-to-suits, where the financial statement of the tenants is critical, this accountant-to-accountant communication works wonders. The tenant's accountant can often explain the profit and net worth picture to the landlord's accountant. Such information is not always immediately understandable without expert background information.

Respect the role of the accountant. His opinions are valuable. He, like the attorney, wants to meet a salesman he can recommend to his clients.

FELLOW BROKERS

Our Realtors' Code of Ethics sets many valuable groundrules for our relations with fellow brokers. It only applies, of course, to those who have agreed to abide by it and who have been accepted as members of the organized real estate community. It is the life blood of the Realtor.

For this, and other reasons, many Realtors will not cooperate unless the cooperating broker is also a Realtor. It may be argued (successfully, I think) that this position is in the best interests of both seller and buyer. It would seem wise, however, to inform your principal of this policy (if you adopt it) as it may not always meet with their approval. If they disapprove of Realtor-only cooperation policy, such principals are always free to deal outside the professional real estate community.

Cooperation

Welcome professional cooperation. The object of taking a listing is to make a sale. It should make no difference who sells the property so long as the transaction is properly handled.

Cooperation is a two-way street. Brokers seeking inventory often want it on a silver platter. They are the send-the-*set-up*-sheet-in-the-mail bunch. The mailing of set-up sheets is a poor policy. How do you know who you're doing business with? How can you be sure he knows enough about the property to sell it? How do you avoid commission split disputes when you do a mail order business?

To serve your seller best, have the cooperating broker come to your office for information. Similarly, go to his office when you want information on one of his listings. Treat the cooperating broker like a buyer. Show him the property just as you'd show it to a buyer. In this way you can be sure your fellow broker will be in the strongest possible position to show the property well.

Don't offer, or seek, cooperation on non-exclusives. The practice of involving, or getting involved with fellow brokers on open or verbal listings causes confusion and controversy. If this practice could be eliminated most of our arbitration committees would have little, or nothing, to do. It's a simple problem to avoid. Just tell all cooperating brokers that you don't want to hear about their non-exclusives. And, of course, keep any opens or verbals you have to yourself.

Remove Uncertainty

Remove all uncertainty from the mind of a cooperating broker. Show him your listing contract. As long as some brokers work on weak arrangements (non-exclusives), there will always be some slight suspicion that you don't have an exclusive. This suspicion often leads to the other broker calling the seller or taking other action to assure himself that you represent the owner. Such action weakens the seller's opinion of all brokers. Don't make it necessary. Be open in your relations with fellow brokers. If you show your contract you'll be able to ask for the same courtesy. This problem does not exist in a strong multiple but not all income listings get on the multiple.

Consider letting the cooperating broker go with you to the seller when he has an offer to present. Most selling brokers want to feel they got a good hearing from the seller. If you let the cooperating broker present his own offer (in your presence) to the seller you'll enjoy the best possible working relationships with the trade. This policy will usually insure that you'll get to present your own offers when you work on other brokers' listings.

Don't get confused as to client relationships. Always work through the cooperating broker. Never contact his client directly without the broker's knowledge and permission.

Protect your own client relationship. Be present during all negotiations. Unless you do this you'll find yourself losing clients to the selling office. Sellers tend to remember the man who sold their property rather than the man who listed it, unless the listing salesman keeps in close touch with them. Besides, the selling office deserves the benefit of your knowledge of and rapport with the seller.

In dealing with other brokers, remember the Golden Rule. It will make your business life both pleasant and profitable.

INSTITUTIONAL LENDERS

It may seem strange to discuss institutional lenders in the same framework as lawyers, accountants and fellow brokers. But these lenders (mutual savings banks, saving and loans, insurance companies) are essential to your success. Many salesmen lose transactions because of their inability to work with a lender. The success-program salesmen often makes that extra one or two sales per year because he knows how to communicate with the lenders. Here are some profit-making tips that will help you put more transactions together.

Preparation

The lender usually has the largest financial interest in the transaction. To advance 60% to 70% of the value in a loan, he must know the property thoroughly. Surprisingly, however, many lenders' staffs are small and overburdened.

You can often make the difference between getting the loan and not getting it simply by your preparation and presentation. Have all the facts as to income and expense at hand and well organized. Do a rental survey to support your income statement. Get the actual income for the last 12 to 24 months from the seller in writing.

Gather some recent comparable sales data and present it with your application. This data ought to include some concrete evidence as to land values, even if you are seeking a loan on improved property.

Provide the lender with square footage rental figures if you are looking for a loan on improved property. Your data ought to show both gross building area and net rentable area. The lender will check your figures, but you'll build confidence by providing this and other information.

Lenders can be sold. It is up to you to sell them your package. You can do this if you prepare properly.

Full Disclosure

Be honest in your dealings with your lender. Point out the less desirable features of the property. It won't hurt you. Every property will support a loan from some lender, so why try to kid any lender along. Most of them can't be fooled and many of them will make a marginal loan if it is honestly presented to them.

Don't play games with the lender. Be frank about the interest rate and points that the buyer has agreed to pay. If the buyer will pay $9\frac{3}{4}\%$ interest (and this is the going rate) don't apply for $9\frac{1}{4}\%$. If you try this you'll find the lender committing at $9\frac{3}{4}\%$ (because that's the current rate) and you'll also find the lender uncovering the fact that the buyer was willing to pay that rate all along. This hurts you in this transaction and all subsequent transactions.

The Application

Go with the buyer when he applies for the loan. This shows the buyer you are vitally interested in him and it shows the lender that you control the buyer and have his complete confidence.

When the lender knows you control the buyer, he will consult with you about any problem. Many of these problems can be worked out without getting the buyer involved and upset.

In all your dealings with a lender, from the application to the funding of the loan, be courteous and be prompt. Treat the lender as you would a client. Respect the value of his time. Be on time for appointments and return his telephone calls promptly. In short, act like a good businessman and you'll be treated like one.

Loan Policy

Most lenders have a carefully worked out loan policy. The area in which they will loan, the per cent of value, the terms, the type of property and their attitude towards secondary financing are all parts of this policy.

Never, never, never, put yourself in the position of making the lender's loan policy for him. There is nothing that alienates a lender faster than the presumptous broker who tries to tell them how to run their business. Guard against making any statement which might be interpreted as an attempt to dictate lender policy.

Try to learn and understand the current policies of your lenders. Work with these policies. Take your transactions where they are welcome. Don't waste time trying to educate a lender.

Know the Loan Market

Discuss your listings with your lenders and get an idea as to who would be interested in making a loan when you sell it. You can't get a firm commitment in the absence of a sale, of course, but you can (by knowing the market) avoid shopping your loan around.

If you stay in touch with the market, you'll eventually settle on two or three lenders. It is wise to concentrate your loan volume. It makes you a valuable customer of the lender. Once in a while he will make a marginal loan (marginal in the sense that it doesn't completely fit into his policy) for a valued broker customer.

We Are Partners

The lender and the broker are in the real estate business together. What hurts one eventually hurts the other.

In time of tight money, brokers are often tempted to advise buyers on methods which will allow them to "go around" a lender. Such advice usually is given to point out how to beat an alienation clause. This is unwise. It can hurt both buyer and seller and it will always hurt you. Not only does it damage your relations with the lender it is likely to involve you in more lawsuits than you care to see.

Welcome the help which can be given to your principals by the other professionals who support our business. If you work honestly and intelligently with attorneys, accountants, fellow brokers, and lenders you will build lasting and profitable relationships.

POINTS TO REMEMBER

—You don't function in a vacuum.
—The real professional enjoys working with other professionals. He advises his client to seek their help.
—Attorneys will make more transactions for you than they'll ever kill.
—Write all documents as if an attorney were involved.
—Always meet the client's attorney.
—Treat the attorney like a client.
—Respect an attorney's time.
—Keep the attorney informed.
—Represent *your* client as vigorously as the attorney represents his.
—To get along with accountants, attorneys, and other professionals, *know what you're talking about.*
—Before you see a client's accountant—prepare.
—Be accurate. Use a calculator.
—Be organized. Use spread sheets.
—Respect an accountant's time.
—Have one accountant talk to another accountant.
—Take some basic accounting courses.
—Cooperate with Realtors.
—Don't mail set-up sheets.
—Treat a cooperating broker like a client.
—Don't offer, or seek cooperation on non-exclusive listings.
—Show the cooperating broker your listing contract.
—To get the most out of lenders: *Be Prepared.*
—Always have some comparable sales data for land values.
—Lenders can be sold.
—Be frank with the lender.
—Go with your buyer to see the lender.
—Respect the lender's time.
—Don't try to make lender policy.

—Stay current. Discuss your listings with your lenders. Don't sell into an impossible loan situation.

—The lender and the broker are partners.

—Never help client's "go around" a lender.

Index